MAHATMA GANDHI
and India's Independence
in World History

Ann Malaspina

E Enslow Publishers, Inc.

40 Industrial Road   PO Box 38
Box 398   Aldershot
Berkeley Heights, NJ 07922 Hants GU12 6BP
USA   UK

http://www.enslow.com

Library of Congress Cataloging-in-Publication Data

Malaspina, Ann, 1957–
    Mahatma Gandhi and India's independence in world history / Ann
Malaspina.
        p. cm.
    Includes bibliographical references (p.) and index.
    Summary: Traces India's struggle to gain independence, highlighting
the life and leadership of Mohandas Gandhi whose tactics of nonviolent
protest have become a goal of resistance movements worldwide.
    ISBN 0-7660-1398-7
    1. Gandhi, Mahatma, 1869–1948. 2. India—Politics and government—
1919–1947. 3. India—History—Autonomy and independence movements.
4. Nationalists—India—Biography. 5. Statesmen—India—Biography.
[1. Gandhi, Mahatma, 1869–1948. 2. India—Politics and government—
1919–1947. 3. India—History. 4. Statesmen.] I. Title.
    DS481.G3 M2747   2000
    954.03'5'092—dc21
                                                            99-050570

Printed in the United States of America

10 9 8 7 6 5 4 3 2 1

To Our Readers:
All Internet addresses in this book were active and appropriate at the time we
went to press. Any comments or suggestions can be sent by e-mail to
Comments@enslow.com or to the address on the back cover.

Illustration Credits: Enslow Publishers, Inc., pp. 6, 101; Library of
Congress, pp. 4, 23, 25, 29, 31, 32, 35, 38, 42, 44, 47, 50, 60, 63, 79, 83, 92,
94, 98, 103, 106, 109, 111, 118, 119.

Cover Illustration: Library of Congress (Gandhi portrait); © Digital
Vision Ltd. (Background).

Contents

1 The Salt March 5

2 Europe Discovers India 12

3 Gandhi's Early Years 28

4 Fighting for Civil Rights in
South Africa 37

5 The Indian National Congress 53

6 Rebellion and Reform 64

7 The Spinning Wheel and Nehru 77

8 Quit India 85

9 A New Nation and the
Death of Gandhi 100

Timeline 120

Chapter Notes 122

Further Reading 126

Index 127

Gandhi (center) during the Salt March on the way to Dandi with some of his followers in 1930.

Chapter 1

The Salt March

Mohandas Karamchand Gandhi leaned down and picked up a pinch of dried sea salt from the beach at Dandi, a small village on the coast in western India. As he held the bit of salt above his head, he was deliberately breaking the law of the British Raj, the colonial government of India. "With this I am shaking the foundations of the British Empire," said Gandhi.[1] Thousands of men and women surrounded him. They knew Gandhi's simple act of defiance would move India a little closer to freedom.

As subjects of the British Empire, the people of India in the spring of 1930 were forced to buy their salt from government salt monopolies. Even those Indians who were too poor to pay the high government tax on salt were not allowed to collect salt from the beaches,

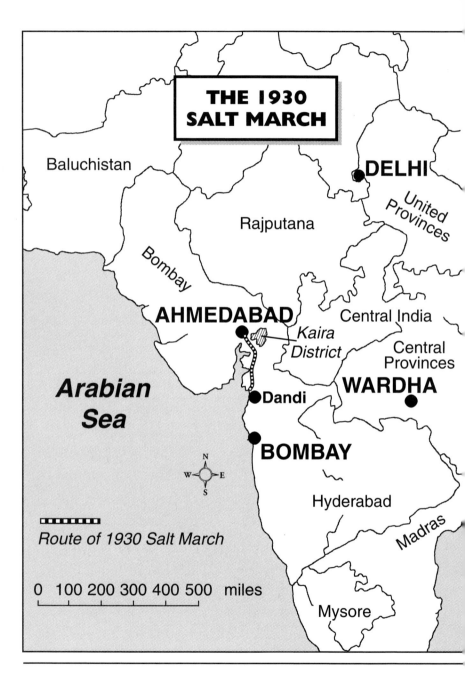

THE 1930 SALT MARCH

Baluchistan

DELHI

United Provinces

Rajputana

Bombay

AHMEDABAD

Kaira District

Central India

Central Provinces

Arabian Sea

Dandi

WARDHA

N
W E
S

BOMBAY

Hyderabad

Route of 1930 Salt March

Madras

0 100 200 300 400 500 miles

Mysore

The Salt March was a 241-mile march to the sea to defy the British tax on salt.

as they had done for generations. Word quickly spread across India that Gandhi and his followers were defying the British salt tax. Soon, thousands of people began walking to the sea with pans to collect salt. Like Gandhi, they believed the salt tax was unfair. They refused to pay it.

Gandhi had begun his protest twenty-four days earlier when he set out on the 241-mile march to the sea. Frail from years of fasting and imprisonment, the sixty-year-old Gandhi left his ashram, or community, in Sabarmati, on foot. He was surrounded by friends and supporters. He was determined to show the British that Indians would no longer pay an unjust tax. Although Gandhi was perhaps the best known person in India, he wore simple white cotton clothes, made of threads spun by hand, to show his support of ordinary Indian peasants. He carried only a bamboo staff to help him on the journey.

As Gandhi and his followers walked along dirt roads through small villages, people threw leaves to welcome them. They knelt in respect as Gandhi passed. At each village, more people joined the march. They were coming together to defy not just the salt tax but British rule of India. When they reached the beach at Dandi on April 5, 1930, and Gandhi leaned down to the sea, several thousand people were at his side.

The Salt Tax

Under the Salt Act of 1882, the British government allowed only government-controlled salt depots to

7

collect and manufacture salt. The British also imposed a tax on salt. Although the tax seemed small, at about forty-six cents on every eighty-two pounds of salt, it posed a hardship for many Indians, who were already struggling to feed their families. Salt was a staple of the Indian diet. It was also a preservative. It helped prevent food from spoiling in the hot climate. The tax affected everyone, but especially India's millions of poor people.

Gandhi wrote a letter to the British viceroy, Lord Edward Wood Irwin. The viceroy was the highest official in India's colonial government. In the letter, dated March 2, 1930, Gandhi warned Irwin that he planned to protest the tax as well as British rule:

> And why do I regard the British rule as a curse? It has impoverished the dumb millions [those Indians who had no voice in the colonial government] by a system of progressive exploitation and by a ruinous expensive military and civil administration which the country can never afford. It has reduced us politically to serfdom [slavery]. It has sapped the foundations of our culture.[2]

Irwin did nothing to stop Gandhi's march. But in the next months, as the peaceful revolt against the salt tax spread across India, the British arrested tens of thousands of protesters. Acting against Gandhi's wishes, some protesters turned to violence. They stoned trains, cut telegraph wires, and even killed some government officials. In Bombay, one of India's largest cities, a crowd of sixty thousand people

Source Document

I want world sympathy in this battle of Right against Might.

Gandhi *MKGandhi*

5ᵗ.4:30

Gandhi wrote this message—"I want world sympathy in this battle of Right against Might"—during the 1930 Salt March.

---

gathered after the police raided an illegal salt-making operation. Many were arrested, including political leaders of the movement to free India from colonial rule. The movement to form an independent nation had been growing for three decades. Jawaharlal Nehru, a close friend of Gandhi's, was sentenced to six months in jail for breaking the Salt Act.

In early May, after Gandhi wrote another letter to the viceroy, threatening to take over the government's Dharasana Saltworks, the British came for Gandhi. He was asleep in his tent near the Dandi beach. Gandhi was not surprised. He went peacefully. The authorities held him without a trial. He would spend his time in prison writing letters and meditating. Gandhi knew the Salt March was just one more step on the road to a self-governing India.

Not everyone agreed with all of Gandhi's ideas, which included not just self-determination for India, but also a new Indian identity and the rejection of many traditional customs and beliefs. However, after nearly two centuries of British rule, India was impatient to be free.

In Gandhi, India had found a unique leader. He wanted India to become an independent and democratic nation. He also sought to challenge India's social order, which had long been divided by class and religion. In efforts like the Salt March, Gandhi tried to lift up the poor, whom he called India's "skeletons." He wanted to provide them with dignity and hope. "He did not descend from the top," wrote Jawaharlal Nehru. "He seemed to emerge from the millions of India, speaking their language and incessantly drawing attention to them and their appalling condition."[3]

The rebellion against the salt tax lasted nearly a year. It ended only after Gandhi and Lord Edward Irwin negotiated a settlement. The Salt March was a significant step on the road to Indian independence from British imperial rule. It showed India's growing discontent. Even the British knew that their time in India was growing short. The question was whether independence would come through peaceful negotiation, as Gandhi wished, or through violence and upheaval.

Chapter 2

Europe Discovers India

The first European known to set foot in India was Portuguese explorer Vasco de Gama in 1498. He recognized that India's calico and spices were valuable trade goods. Portuguese and Dutch traders were soon buying silk, cotton, indigo, grains, and spices cheaply in India to sell for great profits in Europe. In 1600, Queen Elizabeth I granted a charter to a group of traders to create the British East India Company. The charter gave the company a monopoly on the British sea trade in India. The English established a trading port at Surat in 1612.

The East India Company, supported by England's superior naval power, grew to dominate European trade in India. In 1661, Portugal gave the British the western port of Bombay as a gift in exchange for English support against the Dutch. A British captain founded the port settlement of Calcutta on the east coast in 1690. Madras in the southeast became another important British port.

At this time, India was under the rule of the Mughal Empire. Babur, a Muslim leader from Afghanistan, had conquered India in 1526. But as regional Hindu kingdoms emerged under the rule of *maharajas*, or Indian princes, and the East India Company armies became more powerful, the Mughal Empire lost power.

Meanwhile, European traders were not content just to buy India's goods. They wanted to control India itself. In 1689, the East India Company established administrative districts called presidencies in the provinces of Bengal, Madras, and Bombay. Thus, the company began its rule of India.

India's Geography and People

India is separated from the rest of Asia by the Himalaya Mountains, the tallest mountain range in the world. The snow-covered Himalayas are the source of India's three major rivers: the Indus, the Ganges, and the Brahmaputra. Hindus consider the Ganges the holiest river in India.

The vast Indian subcontinent, which today comprises 1.23 million square miles, stretches more than two thousand miles from the Himalayas bordering China and Tibet to the rice paddies of the state of Kerala in the south. Shaped like a diamond, India is surrounded on three sides by water: the Indian Ocean to the south, the Arabian Sea to the west, and the Bay of Bengal to the east. The country contains three major geographical regions: the Himalayas in the north; the Indo-Gangetic plain in central India; and the southern peninsula, known as the Deccan. India contains vast dry deserts, rain forests, fertile farmland, coastal rice paddies, and many other ecosystems.

The British discovered that India's people were as diverse as its geography. Because India had been invaded many times, the people were a melting pot of many different skin colors and physical features. The darker-skinned Indians in the south descended from people known as Dravidians. They had settled in the Indus Valley from about 2400 to 1600 B.C. They were pushed south when the lighter-skinned Aryan nomads from Europe and the Middle East invaded India in 1500 B.C. Isolated northern tribes near the border of Tibet and Burma resembled their Chinese neighbors.

The Indians did not share a common language. Nearly 190 languages and 544 dialects have been identified in India. Today, at least 225 regional dialects and eighteen major languages are spoken. The languages include Hindi (modern India's official language), Bengali, Punjabi, Tamil, Urdu, Kashmiri, Sanskrit, and English.

Indians ate different food, depending on the climate and agricultural products of their regions. Unlike many countries, India did not have one unifying national religion.

Hinduism

Despite centuries of Muslim rule, the majority of Indians were Hindus. Hinduism, a way of life as well as a religion, was developed by the Aryan nomads who migrated into northwest India around 1500 B.C. Hinduism has no founder or prophet, nor a single set of beliefs. Rather, as the religion emerged over centuries, it absorbed many philosophies and practices.

Hindus worship many gods and goddesses. The three most important Hindu gods are Brahma the Creator, Vishnu the Preserver, and Shiva the Destroyer. Together, the three gods symbolize the Brahman, the ultimate god. Hindus also worship gods and goddesses associated with the elements, like fire and water. Other Hindu deities represent plants and animals, as well as concepts like art, wealth, and happiness.

Hindus believe that people must be reincarnated, or reborn, many times before achieving spiritual salvation, or freedom from rebirth. Only good *karma* (Sanskrit for action or deeds) will lead to this desired state. A Hindu must also follow his or her *dharma* (a Sanskrit word referring to a person's duties). Ceremonies for each stage of life, from birth to death, are important to Hinduism. For example, Hindus cremate their dead so that their ashes can be thrown into the sacred river, the Ganges.

Hindus are very conscious of cleanliness. Because they believe the soul can take many shapes, even that of animals, Hindus generally do not eat meat, especially beef. They believe cows are sacred and should not be killed. Cows are allowed to wander freely. They are often seen on city streets, market-places, even beaches. Many Hindus, including Gandhi, practice the principle of *ahimsa*. This Buddhist concept means nonviolence to living creatures.

The Hindus' beliefs are collected in the Vedas, scriptures passed down orally for centuries. The Vedas were written in Sanskrit, the classical sacred and literary language of the Hindus, between 1000 B.C. and A.D. 500. During Gandhi's life, about three quarters of India's population were Hindu. Today, about 82 percent of Indians are Hindus.

Islam in India

Muslims, followers of the Islamic religion, have also profoundly influenced India's history and culture. Islam is the second largest religion in India. Unlike Hindus, Muslims believe in one God, Allah. Islam was founded by the prophet Mohammed in Mecca on the west coast of the Arabian peninsula around A.D. 610. The Muslim calendar dates from A.D. 622, when Mohammed was expelled from Mecca because of his teachings and fled about three hundred miles north to Medina. Mohammed is regarded by Muslims as the last of the prophets who revealed the word of God through the Koran, the Islamic holy book.

Muslims from Turkey and Afghanistan invaded Northern India around the year A.D. 1000. Muhammad of Ghur, whose reign began in 1173, is considered the founder of Muslim power in India. Muslim leaders, called sultans, lived in Delhi and ruled all of northern India by 1200.

New Muslim invaders, the Mughals, crossed into India from central Asia in 1526. Led by Babur, the powerful Mughal Army rode horses and carried guns. The Muslims quickly defeated the Indian Army. Mughal emperors ruled much of India for centuries. They introduced an advanced society with great art and culture. Many magnificent Islamic buildings, like the Taj Mahal in Agra, still stand. The Mughal Empire declined after the arrival of European traders. It ended in 1858. Today, about 12 percent of Indians are Muslims.

Other Indian Religions

Many religions have begun on Indian soil. Buddhism was founded in Northern India in about 500 B.C., when Siddhartha Guatama, an Indian prince, found enlightenment, a new understanding of life that halts the sequence of birth and death. Siddhartha preached love, compassion, tolerance, and self-restraint. Buddhism, the fourth largest religion in the world, flourishes today in many Asian countries. But in India, Buddhism was displaced by Hinduism. Only 0.7 percent of Indians today are Buddhists. However, many Buddhist principles, like ahimsa, are integrated in Indian thought.

Also in the sixth century B.C., Jainism was started in India by a Hindu reformer named Vardhamana.

Jainism is an ascetic religion. (Ascetics deny themselves the usual pleasures of life.) Jains follow a strict moral code and believe in nonviolence. They avoid killing even insects. Some Jains wear cloth masks to avoid killing germs when they breathe. Only about 3 million Jains live in India today.

Another important Indian religion, Sikhism (from the Sanskrit word *shiksh*, which means to learn), was created by the mystic Nanak, who lived from 1469 to 1539. Nanak wanted to unite Muslims and Hindus. All Sikh men use the last name Singh. They never cut their hair, which they wear wrapped in a turban. They carry a knife, and wear a steel bangle on their right wrist and a special undergarment. Sikhism absorbed parts of Islam and Hinduism. Unlike Hindus, Sikhs believe in one god. Today, India is home to more than 16 million Sikhs.

Christianity also has a rich history on the Indian subcontinent. European missionaries discovered Christian Indians in southern India. These Indians claimed that St. Thomas founded their church in the first century A.D. Christians in Kerala and Madras were probably converted in the second or third century A.D. Saint Francis Xavier, a Spanish missionary, came to Goa in 1542. He converted thousands of Indians along the west coast and in South India and Ceylon. Portuguese and English missionaries also sought to convert Indians. Relatively small Christian communities thrive today in Goa, Kerala, and other regions. Kerala in South India also contains one of the oldest Jewish communities in the world.

The Caste System

Over many centuries, a caste system, or social order, developed among Hindus. The Aryans who established Hinduism divided society into four *varnas* (Sanskrit for color), or castes. People whose skin was lighter were generally assigned to higher castes. The *Brahman* caste of priests, religious leaders, and scholars was the most revered group. Beneath the *Brahmans* were the *Kshatriyas*, the wealthy landowners, warriors, and political rulers. The *Vaisya* caste of farm landowners, traders, and merchants made up the middle class. The *Sudras* were the servants, craftsmen, and laborers. Over many centuries, marriages between invaders and Indians produced many thousands of subcastes.

The caste system provided order in Hindu society. Each caste had its place in the community, giving people both a sense of identity and an occupation. A person was born into the caste of his or her parents. Thus, the son of a shopkeeper who sold silk goods would grow up to do the same. Traditionally, Hindus were not supposed to marry outside their caste. The daughter of a Brahman could not marry the son of a potter without risking rejection by her family and community. In theory, Hindus still live by the rules of caste, although occupations are no longer strictly determined by caste, especially among educated persons in cities.

People called untouchables ranked below the four main castes. They were considered unclean by caste Indians, although not in the physical sense. Rather, they were close to things that Hindus believed were polluting, such as death and human waste. Brahmans kept themselves away from such things. Untouchables were assigned the lowest occupations. Their jobs, however, were essential to the community. They swept the streets, collected garbage, cleaned people's waste, and cremated the dead. Because they were viewed as unclean, untouchables were forbidden to speak to, touch, or look at a caste member. A Brahman would not eat food handled by an untouchable. Shunned by society and desperately poor, untouchables were banned from Hindu temples and were not allowed to drink from public wells.

Gandhi respected the caste system for its social structure. But he was horrified at the discrimination against untouchables. He called untouchability "a sin and the greatest blot on Hinduism."[1] Gandhi worked for many years to improve the social status of untouchables. Today, untouchables have legal rights and protections as Indian citizens. Still, attitudes have been slow to change. Many untouchables call themselves *Dalits*, which means "The Oppressed."

Expansion of British Rule

India's varied population, its divisions into areas ruled by Hindu princes and kingdoms ruled by Mughals, and its huge size allowed the British to seize power easily.

There was no unified opposition. The East India Company overpowered local rulers, then forced them to pay taxes in return for protection and services. The company fought battles against the maharajas and turned the princes against each other.

France was also a colonial power in India. But England and France were bitter enemies. They were fighting for control of India and other countries around the globe. In 1757, Robert Clive led the East India Company troops in the Battle of Plassey, winning victory over France. The East India Company was now the leading power in India. Warren Hastings of the East India Company became the first governor-general of India. The British colonial era had begun.

Beyond controlling the ports, the English in India spread British culture, values, and ideas. Lord Thomas Macaulay, a member of the British Parliament (legislature) in the 1830s, proposed the revolutionary idea that India should not remain permanently under the domination of the European traders. This could be accomplished, he believed, by giving Indians an English education and helping their economy.

British Influence Grows

Gradually, the British began to put their moral and cultural stamp on India. They believed that their European and Protestant values were superior to those of the Hindus and Muslims in India. They wanted to "civilize" the Indian natives.

The British, for example, were shocked at the Hindu custom of *sati*. In this custom, widows join their dead husbands on the funeral pyre. A Hindu wife was expected to end her life with her husband's death. She threw herself, often involuntarily, into the fire in which her husband's body was burning. In 1829, the British banned sati. Other Hindu customs, such as child marriage, were also banned or discouraged by the British.

English replaced Persian, the ancient language of India, as the official language of the Indian government in 1828. Schools and colleges were built to teach Indians English literature and Western culture. Students were no longer instructed in Indian languages and Indian history. Christian missionaries converted Hindus and Muslims.

The Sepoy Rebellion

The British conquest of India was completed with the defeat of Sikh rebellions in the Punjab and Sind regions of northern India in the 1840s. But India's discontent was awakening.

The first mass uprising against the British occurred in 1857. Many Hindu and Muslim soldiers, or *sepoys*, served in the East India Company's army. The sepoys resented the British disregard for Indian culture. They were often sent overseas to fight Great Britain's wars, even though Hindus considered crossing seas polluting. Tensions mounted when the new Lee-Enfield rifle was introduced in the 1850s. To load the rifles, soldiers had to bite open the cartridges, which were rumored

The Sepoy Rebellion was the first attempt by native Indians to overthrow British imperial rule. The rebellion was brutally put down.

to be greased with pork fat and beef fat. Hindus do not eat beef, and Muslims do not eat pork. The rifles proved to be a breaking point.

The Sepoy Rebellion erupted on May 10, 1857, in Meerut, a town northeast of Delhi. The sepoys quickly took control of Delhi. The last Mughal emperor, Bahadur Shah, supported the rebels. Violence spread across northern India. Many died on both sides before the British crushed the rebels a year later.

Shocked by the bloody revolt, the British government passed the Act for the Better Government of

India in 1858. This marked an important turning point in Indian history. The British Crown took control of the Indian territories held by the East India Company. The East India Company's twenty-four-thousand-man army was made part of the British Army. In 1874, the East India Company was dissolved.

Maharajas

During the period of British rule, about one fifth of the Indian population was ruled by 562 Indian maharajas. These wealthy Indian royals had inherited their titles and land. They ruled the peasants who lived on their land, who comprised about one third of India's population. Many of the maharajas were educated in elite British schools. The British allowed the maharajas to keep their land, which was called India's princely states.

The princes made laws and levied taxes. The British gave them titles to enhance their status and to keep them loyal. But the Indian royals had little authority. They could not conduct foreign policy or fight with other states. The Raj could supervise succession when a prince died.

Queen Victoria

In 1867, Great Britain's Queen Victoria was named empress of India. She was truly fond of India. She studied Hindi, the most common Indian language. Queen Victoria employed Indian servants and had a trusted Indian Muslim advisor named Abdul Karim. During the Victorian Era, from 1837 to 1901, Great

Queen Victoria, the leader of Great Britain during the first years of British rule in India, was named empress of India.

Britain became the richest and most powerful nation in the world. Its colonies included one quarter of the world. By the time Queen Victoria died in 1901, many of those colonies, including India, were impatient for freedom.

The Economics of Colonialism

Economic stress helped ignite India's revolt against British rule. For many decades, British traders and industrialists used India's raw materials and labor for profit. The peasants paid high taxes to the British, as they had paid to the Mughal emperors and maharajas before them. By the end of the nineteenth century, many Indians believed that the British had exploited India's people and drained India's natural resources for too long.

Great Britain did introduce modern improvements to India, from railroads to libraries. But the colonial

Source Document

So far as I am able to judge, nothing has been left undone, either by man or nature, to make India the most extraordinary country that the sun visits on his round. Nothing seems to have been forgotten, nothing overlooked.[2]

American writer Mark Twain went to India in 1896 to write about the country. He called India the "Land of Wonder."

relationship created within India an imbalanced society in which a person's skin color, language, and religion determined his or her civil rights. According to Gandhi biographer Louis Fischer, "The British were masters in somebody else's house. Their very presence was a humiliation."[3]

Chapter 3

Gandhi's Early Years

India was Great Britain's largest and most important colony when Mohandas Karamchand Gandhi was born on October 2, 1869. While Great Britain reaped wealth and prestige from the "Jewel in the Crown," as India was called, the majority of India's 250 million people were poor, illiterate farmers. Gandhi, however, enjoyed a comfortable childhood. He grew up in Porbandar, one of the smallest of India's princely states. It was a small city of white buildings and Hindu temples on the Kathiawar Peninsula on India's west coast.

The Gandhis were a prominent family. Gandhi's father, Karamchand, was the *dewan,* or prime minister, to the maharaja of Porbandar. The dewan ran the local government and represented the prince to British officials.

Karamchand Gandhi, Mohandas Gandhi's father, was a respected political official.

Karamchand, who inherited his post from Gandhi's grandfather, Uttamchand, was greatly admired for his diplomatic skills. "[H]e was incorruptible and had earned a name for strict impartiality in his family as well as outside. His loyalty to the state was well known," Gandhi wrote later.[1] Gandhi's uncle, Tulsidas, became dewan after Karamchand moved on to work for another maharaja in the state of Rajkot.

Gandhi was the fourth child of Karamchand's fourth wife, Putlibai. Karamchand's first three wives had died. The Gandhi family lived in a three-story stone house. It had a small courtyard, surrounded by a high wall. The house still stands today. They shared the simple home with Gandhi's five uncles on his father's side and their families.

Gandhi's parents were not formally educated. Still, books on religion and mythology filled the home. "My father never had any ambition to accumulate riches and left us very little property. He had no education, save that of experience," wrote Gandhi.[2]

Gandhi as a Young Student

Gandhi spent his first years of school at the *dhooli shala*, or dust school, in Porbandar. With no desks, paper, pencils, or chalkboards, the teacher and students copied letters and numbers on the sand floor. Gandhi was an unexceptional student. "It was with some difficulty that I got through the multiplication tables," he later recalled.[3]

Gandhi, seen here at the age of seven, was a poor student who was terribly shy.

Gandhi was not very studious, and his shyness left him with few friends. "He seemed to have little ability and less talent," noted Gandhi biographer Louis Fischer.[4] Being small and slight, Gandhi was not interested in sports such as cricket and gymnastics. Instead, he formed a lifelong habit of walking, which helped him stay healthy and strong. He also enjoyed reading books.

A Hindu Family

Like the majority of Indians, the Gandhi family was Hindu. Hinduism's many rituals and customs influenced all aspects of Gandhi's life. The Gandhi family belonged to the Vaisya, or merchant, caste and the Bania subcaste. Like many Hindus, Gandhi was raised vegetarian. He once rebelled and ate a bite of goat meat offered to him by a Muslim schoolmate. He became sick and later dreamed of a live goat in his stomach. "I . . . knew that, if my mother and father came to know of my having become a meat-eater, they would be deeply shocked. This knowledge was

Putlibai, Gandhi's mother, was a devoutly religious woman whose beliefs would have a profound effect on her son.

gnawing at my heart," he wrote.[5] He was determined never to eat meat again.

Gandhi's mother, Putlibai, prayed at the Hindu temple every day. "The outstanding impression my mother has left on my memory is that of saintliness. She was deeply religious. She would not think of taking her meals without her daily prayers," wrote Gandhi.[6] Putlibai frequently fasted for religious reasons. One year at Chaturmas, the four-month rainy season that is a time of fasting for Hindus, she promised not to eat until she saw the sun, Gandhi recalled.

His mother's fasts made a lasting impression on Gandhi. As an adult, he frequently fasted to purify his body and to prove his self-discipline. By denying his body's needs, Gandhi believed his soul's power would increase and he would give strength to the world. Gandhi also fasted as a political weapon to persuade the British government to listen to his demands.

Early Marriage

When Gandhi was seven, the family moved to Rajkot, one hundred miles north of Porbandar.

Source Document

We children on those days would stand, staring at the sky, waiting to announce the appearance of the sun to our mother. . . . I remember days when, at [the sun's] sudden appearance, we would rush and announce it to her. She would run out to see with her own eyes, but by that time the fugitive sun would be gone, thus depriving her of her meal. "That does not matter," she would say cheerfully. "God did not want me to eat today."[7]

Gandhi's mother's deep religious faith compelled her to fast, just as Gandhi himself would do as an adult. Here, Gandhi recalled one of her fasts.

There, Karamchand was appointed dewan to the maharaja of Rajkot. Gandhi attended the Alfred High School in Rajkot. At age thirteen, Gandhi married a thirteen-year-old girl named Kasturbhai Makanji. As is common in Hindu families, the two sets of parents arranged the marriage. Later, Gandhi denounced the ancient Hindu custom of child marriages. "I can see no moral argument in support of such a preposterously early marriage," he wrote.[8]

After the lavish Hindu wedding ceremony in 1882, Kasturbhai moved into the Gandhi household. She was the daughter of a Porbandar merchant. Like many

Indian women of her time, she never learned to read. She was devoted to Gandhi and shared in his life's work. Yet as the years passed, she occasionally rebelled against some of his unconventional ideas.

Gandhi admired his wife's fearlessness. As a teenager, Gandhi was afraid of the dark. He was haunted by fears of thieves, ghosts, and serpents. "I knew that she had more courage than I, and I felt ashamed of myself. . . . She could go out anywhere in the dark," he wrote.[9]

Gandhi Studies in London

When Gandhi's father died in 1885, he left little property or money to his heirs. His job as dewan had given him status but not wealth. After graduating from high school, Gandhi decided to go to England to study law. His family felt that Gandhi should get an English law degree so that he could one day take his father's position as dewan of Rajkot. But his caste elders in Bombay believed that crossing oceans was polluting to Hindus. They felt he could not practice Hinduism in England. They forbade him to go. Determined to set his own course, however, on September 4, 1888, Gandhi said good-bye to his wife and newborn son, Harilal. He boarded a steamship for the three-week trip to Southampton, England.

In London, Gandhi studied French, Latin, physics, chemistry, and law. He also tried to improve his English. He felt like an outsider, but he tried to fit in with British society. He even shed his Indian dress to

As a law student in London, Gandhi took to wearing fancy clothes, to fit in better with his European classmates.

look more like an English gentleman. "He bought a top hat, spats, striped trousers, a morning coat, a silver-mounted cane, silk shirts, and leather gloves," biographer Louis Fischer wrote.[10]

At the same time, Gandhi became more aware of his own culture. Much of the English diet of meat and dairy products was forbidden to devout Hindus. Remembering his vow to his mother to remain a vegetarian, Gandhi decided to cook his own meals, including his specialty, carrot soup. He also joined the Vegetarian Society of England.

Learning About Religion

He began to read the Old and New Testaments and the *Bhagavad Gita,* or Celestial Song, the sacred Hindu book. Written between the fifth and second centuries B.C., the Bhagavad Gita is a conversation between Krishna, the human embodiment of the Hindu god Vishnu, and Arjuna, an archer and fighter, during a famous battle, the *Mahabharata.* Arjuna, fighting his cousins, asks Krishna whether he is justified in killing his own kin. Krishna reminds Arjuna of his duty as a warrior. By fulfilling his dharma, he upholds law and order and saves the kingdom from unrighteous rulers. The Bible and the Bhagavad Gita formed the basis of much of Gandhi's philosophy.

Early Career of a Young Lawyer

Gandhi officially became a lawyer on June 10, 1891. Two days later, he sailed for Bombay. On his return to India, Gandhi learned that his mother had died. Adding to his troubles, his first trial as a lawyer was an embarrassing failure. He never tried another case in India. When a Muslim business firm in Porbandar proposed to send him to South Africa to conduct legal work, Gandhi seized the opportunity. With that decision, Gandhi began an important new chapter in his life.

Gandhi had grown up protected by his family's social status. But his London law degree and middle-class upbringing could not shield him from the racial discrimination he would find in South Africa.

Soon, he would be leading nonviolent protests to win civil rights for Indian immigrants there. According to biographer Judith M. Brown, Gandhi's two decades in South Africa would see "the transformation of the timid, failed barrister [lawyer] into a skilled lawyer, political spokesman and organizer, equipped to play a public role in India."[11]

While he was away, India would begin its long journey to independence.

Chapter 4

Fighting for Civil Rights in South Africa

On a cold night in 1893, Gandhi sat alone on a hard wooden bench in a train station in Maritzburg. The capital of Natal, Maritzburg was located on the east coast of South Africa. Forced off the train because he refused to give up his first-class seat and move into the van compartment with the other Indian passengers, Gandhi watched his train to Pretoria pull out of the station. Gandhi held a first-class ticket, but because of his dark skin, the railroad rules forbade him from sitting with white passengers in the best seats.

Gandhi boarded the train earlier that day on his way to his new job. As Gandhi later recalled, a fellow passenger complained to train officials that Gandhi was sitting with the white passengers:

"But I have a first class ticket," said I [Gandhi].
"That doesn't matter," rejoined the other [a train official]. "I tell you, you must go to the van compartment."[1]

When Gandhi refused, a constable took him by the hand and pushed him out of the train entirely. As the train steamed away, he sat alone on a bench in the station. He was too scared to get his coat from his luggage. ". . . I did not dare to ask for it lest I should be insulted again, so I sat and shivered," Gandhi wrote.[2]

Gandhi came to South Africa to work as a lawyer. However, he quickly saw a larger purpose. "I saw that South Africa was no country for a self-respecting Indian, and my mind became more and more occupied with the question as to how this state of things might be improved," he recalled later.[3] In the process, Gandhi discovered his talents as a leader. He also learned the power of civil disobedience as a weapon for social change.

Colonization of South Africa

The European takeover of South Africa began in

Gandhi, as he looked during the early years of his legal practice in South Africa.

1652. The Dutch East India Company, a trading group, set up a fort and provision station at the Cape of Good Hope on the southern tip of Africa. The trading station grew to become the Cape Colony.

During the next hundred years, the Dutch, French, and Germans took over the region from the native Africans. They settled as farmers and sheep and cattle ranchers. Many Africans died of smallpox and other previously unknown diseases brought by the Europeans. The Europeans overpowered the Africans with superior weapons. Those Africans who survived lost their land. They became subjects of the white settlers.

In the early 1800s, the British began gaining territory in South Africa. In 1814, the British purchased the Cape Colony from the Dutch for £6 million, the English currency. After 1820, thousands of English colonists arrived in the Cape Colony. English became the official language. The British abolished slavery and gave Africans limited civil rights. The Dutch settlers, known as Afrikaners or Boers (the Dutch word for farmers), resented the British dominance. They moved inland across the Orange River into lands occupied by African tribes.

The Boers defeated the Zulu and other native tribes and created Afrikaner republics called the Orange Free State and the Transvaal. The Boers and British fought over these regions, particularly the Transvaal. Meanwhile, the British established another republic, known as Natal, on the east coast.

Indian Immigrants

Another group of settlers came to South Africa in the 1860s. These were Indians, shipped across the Indian Ocean to work as indentured servants on British sugar and coffee plantations in Natal. Indentured servants must work to pay for their passage to a new place. Many of the Indians were untouchables. They were poor and had little choice but to go with the British. They were paid about five dollars a month and given free room and board to work long hours in the fields. After five years of labor, the Indians were free to return home or to remain in South Africa.

By the 1890s, many Indians in South Africa had worked their way out of servitude to become paid laborers. Still, they remained poor, uneducated, and unskilled. Indian Muslim traders also immigrated to South Africa. Since they competed with the white merchants for business, the whites resented their presence. Indian clerks, doctors, lawyers, and teachers formed a third group among the small South Asian community.

The train officials considered Gandhi just one more Indian immigrant that night in Maritzburg. He boarded the next train for Pretoria in the Transvaal. The following morning, he sent a telegram to the general manager of the railroad, protesting his discriminatory treatment. Gandhi's complaints were apparently heard. He was allowed to sit in first class on the next leg of his journey.

Gandhi Leads Protests

Soon after arriving in Pretoria, Gandhi organized regular meetings of the Indian settlers. He was curious to learn about the social, economic, and political conditions of the Indians. Relations were tense between Indians and whites, both minorities in South Africa. The whites referred to Indians by the derogatory term *coolie.*

In the Orange Free State, Indians had few legal rights. They could work only as waiters or in other menial jobs. Indian traders were driven away by white settlers who would not do business with them. Indians had to pay a fee to enter the Transvaal. Like the African natives, Indians were unable to own property or run businesses in either white-run state. Excluded from politics, Indians were discriminated against in daily life, especially by the Boers. They were not allowed on the streets after 9:00 P.M. without a permit. Nor could they walk down the street with a white person.

Gandhi learned that the Natal government was proposing a Franchise Amendment Bill. It would deprive Indians of the right to vote. Gandhi felt Indians should have the same rights as any British subject. Although Gandhi and his friends realized that the law would probably pass, they sent telegrams to government officials. They also sent a petition with ten thousand signatures to the Colonial Office in London. Despite their actions, the bill became law.

Gandhi (back row, fourth from left) and the other founders of the Natal Indian Congress posed for this photograph in 1895.

With Gandhi's leadership and support from Indian businessmen, the Indians soon became organized. Gandhi formed the Natal Indian Congress in 1894 to debate current issues and unite the Indian community. He created the Transvaal Indian Congress in 1904.

Gandhi earned his living by working for merchants. On the side, he offered free legal advice to the poor. No longer the shy schoolboy, Gandhi spent much of his time writing letters and pamphlets about the unjust treatment of Indians that were distributed in England, India, and South Africa. Gandhi also wanted to improve sanitation and education for Indians. Although black South Africans, forced to live in segregated areas and limited in the jobs they could take, were in many ways worse off than the Indians, Gandhi focused on the problems of Indians.

Indian Ambulance Corps

Throughout the nineteenth century, the English and the Boers struggled for power and wealth in South Africa. The Transvaal Boers defeated the British in the First Boer War in 1880 and 1881. Then, in 1884, gold was discovered in southern Transvaal. English miners moved in, creating the city of Johannesburg. The Boer government began taxing the English heavily. The English revolted in 1895, but failed to overthrow the Transvaal government. In 1899, the Transvaal and Orange Free State declared war against the British in the Second Boer War.

Despite Gandhi's pacifism and opposition to British policy toward Indians, he joined the empire's war effort by forming an ambulance corps. The eleven hundred Indians in the ambulance corps brought stretchers to the battlefields to carry out the wounded. They also worked in hospitals. Gandhi believed that, if Indians proved their loyalty to Great Britain, the British might reward them with more civil rights. For his bravery, the British government awarded Gandhi the War Medal.

The British won the war in 1902. The Transvaal and Orange Free State were granted self-government

Gandhi (middle row, third from right) is seen here with other members of the Indian Ambulance Corps during the Boer War in 1899.

as colonies of the British Empire. Many Boers remained in the governments. Cape Colony and Natal were already British colonies. But Indians were still without civil rights. The Boer general, Louis Botha, who became the first prime minister of independent South Africa, supported the anti-Indian policies. "If my party is returned to office we will undertake to drive the coolies out of the country within four years," he said at an election rally in 1907.[4]

Gandhi, the Private Man

In 1896, Gandhi traveled to India to visit his family. He returned to South Africa with his wife, Kasturbhai, and their two sons, Harilal and Manilal, born in 1892. Gandhi's sister's son also accompanied them. Two more sons would be born in South Africa: Ramdas in 1897, and Devadas in 1900.

When the boat carrying Gandhi's family arrived at the Durban port, a group of whites tried to stop the passengers from disembarking. They did not want more Indians, especially Gandhi, who was well known by then, to enter Natal.

When he was finally allowed ashore, Gandhi was pelted with stones, bricks, and rotten eggs. "Someone snatched away my turban, whilst others began to batter and kick me," he recalled.[5] He was saved by the police, who escorted him home. Gandhi refused to prosecute his assailants.

A Life of Simplicity

In South Africa, Gandhi formed his philosophy of self-reliance, simplicity, and daily labor. In 1904, he bought ninety acres of land outside Durban and established an ashram called Phoenix Farm. An ashram is a community where people live and work together like an extended family. Living simply in tents, the ashram members farmed the rich soil and orchards. They also published the newspaper *Indian Opinion* on a printing press in a small shed.

Gandhi and Kasturbhai would live much of their lives in ashrams. In 1910, Gandhi founded the Tolstoy Farm near Durban. It was a cooperative colony for Indians based on the philosophy of the Russian writer Leo Tolstoy, who advocated self-sufficiency.

Wanting to become self-reliant, Gandhi did his own washing and ironing. He also taught himself basic medical practices. He even delivered his youngest son. He also began fasting some days. On other days he lived on two simple meals of unseasoned nuts and fruits.

Many of Gandhi's unconventional ideas affected the people closest to him, especially Kasturbhai. During this era, most Indians relied on servants, usually untouchables, to do household tasks such as emptying chamber pots. But Gandhi disapproved of giving the worst jobs to servants. He asked Kasturbhai and the other women to empty the chamber pots. Horrified at such a request, Kasturbhai at first refused. She was raised in a traditional Hindu household, where members of high castes would never do this work. But she finally yielded to Gandhi's wishes.

Throughout her life, Kasturbhai had to conform to Gandhi's unconventional beliefs. When Kasturbhai first came to South Africa, Gandhi asked her to wear shoes and stockings, rather than sandals on bare feet. Gandhi himself wore a European suit and an Indian turban. "I believed . . . that in order to look civilized, our dress and manners had as far as possible to

Gandhi's work and lifestyle could be hard on all the members of his immediate family, seen here.

approximate to the European standard," he wrote.[6] Later, Gandhi told his wife to sell her jewelry—an important part of a Hindu woman's identity—to raise funds for his causes.

In 1906, Gandhi took a vow of celibacy. This meant that he would not engage in sexual relations. Celibacy, or *Brahmacharaya*, is an ancient Hindu tradition. It is practiced by older men who choose to renounce all worldly things. Gandhi believed that Brahmacharaya is a search for Brahma, or God. Celibacy for Gandhi was just one aspect of a life that embraced discipline and self-control.

The Black Act and *Satyagraha*

Meanwhile, the Indian community in South Africa faced new restrictions. In 1906, the Transvaal government drafted the Asiatic Law Amendment Ordinance, known as the Black Act. Directed at Indians, it would deny them civil rights and discourage immigration. The law required all Indians over age eight to be fingerprinted and to carry a registration card. If they refused, they would risk deportation. Indians worried that similar laws would spread to the Orange Free State, the Cape Colony, and Natal. Perhaps Indians would be forced to leave South Africa.

On September 11, 1906, Gandhi organized a meeting at the Empire Theater in Johannesburg. Some three thousand Indians crowded into the building. Muslim merchant Sheth Haji Habib read a resolution calling for Indians to refuse to register. Gandhi stood to speak. "The government has taken leave of all sense of decency," he declared. But he warned that Indians who defied the law had to be willing to suffer the consequences. "We may have to go to jail, where we may be insulted. We may have to go hungry and suffer extreme heat or cold. Hard labour may be imposed upon us," he cautioned.[7] Moved by Gandhi's words, the entire audience raised their hands in a pledge to disobey the law.

Gandhi traveled to London. There, he convinced British officials not to approve the law. However, the Transvaal was granted self-government in January 1907. The new Transvaal government passed the Black Act. It became law in July 1907.

In response, Gandhi launched his first civil disobedience campaign, using a technique he called *satyagraha*, a Sanskrit word. *Satya* means truth and love; *agraha* means firmness or force. *Satyagraha* is often translated as "truth force." Satyagraha meant actively standing up against wrong, even risking injury or jail, without resorting to violence. Gandhi would use satyagraha throughout his life to push for change.

Indians surrounded registration offices, plastered streets with posters, and tried to convince fellow Indians not to register under the Black Act. They published the names of those Indians who did so in a local newspaper. The government extended the time limit for registration, but the Indians continued to resist. Finally, the government decided to stop the protests.

In January 1908, government police arrested Gandhi for failing to register. Because he had deliberately broken the law, he asked the judge to give him the most severe penalty—six months of hard labor and a fine of five hundred pounds, the Transvaal currency. The judge sentenced him to two months in prison without hard labor.

Faced with rising social unrest, former Boer General Jan Christiaan Smuts, now the minister in charge of Indian Affairs, agreed to release the prisoners and repeal the Black Act if the Indians would register voluntarily. Gandhi accepted this compromise, but some Indians felt he was a traitor. When Gandhi walked to the registration office to give

General Jan Christiaan Smuts was Gandhi's main adversary in South Africa.

his fingerprints, three or four Indians assaulted him, leaving him unconscious on the street. Resistance increased. The government decided not to repeal the act.

On August 16, 1908, two thousand Indians, led by Gandhi, burned their registration certificates in a public bonfire. On October 7, Gandhi was put in jail for not carrying a registration card and refusing to give his fingerprints. He spent his time in prison reading American writer Henry David Thoreau's essay "On the Duty of Civil Disobedience."

Gandhi was released in December 1908, only to be arrested again in February 1909 in Johannesburg. Again, he was charged with failing to carry a registration certificate. Gandhi was freed in May.

The next month, he traveled to England to speak with government officials about the South African situation. But he made no progress. On his return trip, Gandhi wrote an important document called *Hind Swaraj* (Indian Freedom). In it, Gandhi laid out his ideas about India's independence from England. "If we act justly India will be free sooner . . . if we are just

to them (the British), we shall receive their support,"
he wrote.[8]

Indian Relief Act

Great Britain granted South Africa independence in
1910. The Union of South Africa was created. But the
new constitution gave whites almost complete power.
Life for Indians as well as black South Africans did not
improve. New laws levied special taxes on Indians,
restricted Indian immigration, and said that only
Christian marriages were legal. In protest, Gandhi led
a satyagraha campaign from 1913 to 1914.

The British realized that they could not ignore
Gandhi. In 1914, Gandhi and General Jan Smuts
negotiated the Indian Relief Bill. It recognized Hindu
and Muslim marriages and lifted unfair taxes on
Indians. But other injustices remained. Still, Gandhi
was pleased enough to send General Smuts a pair of
sandals he had made in prison. The Boer leader wore
the sandals for many years.

World War I

World War I began in 1914. On June 28, 1914, a Serb
assassinated Archduke Franz Ferdinand, heir to the
throne of Austria-Hungary, in Sarajevo, Bosnia. The
intense nationalism—the desire for countries to rule
themselves—sweeping through Europe at the time
quickly turned a regional crisis into a global war
involving thirty-two nations.

When Great Britain entered World War I on
August 4, 1914, India, as a British colony, also went to

war. More than a million Anglo-Indian troops fought with the Allies—France, Russia, Italy, and the United States—against the Central Powers—Germany, Austria-Hungary, Turkey, and Bulgaria. Gandhi traveled to London and formed an ambulance corps of Indians in England. But he became seriously ill with pleurisy, a lung inflammation.

Gandhi and Kasturbhai decided that it was time for them to return permanently to India. Gandhi had accomplished much in his twenty-one years in South Africa. However, his dream of equal rights for Indians there would not be realized for more than seventy years.

Chapter 5

The Indian National Congress

While Gandhi campaigned for civil rights in South Africa, political and social unrest was escalating in India. The new Indian middle class was leading the way. This "dynamic minority" had "a sense of unity, of purpose, and of hope. It was the newborn soul of modern India," wrote historian Vincent A. Smith.[1] Rather than the wealthy maharajas or the poor masses, these men and women would invent India's future.

Many of the lawyers, merchants, writers, teachers, and government employees of the middle class were educated in English schools and colleges in England and India. They spoke and wrote fluent English. Thus, a teacher from Bombay could communicate in English with a lawyer from Calcutta, even though their native languages were different. They followed political developments in new Indian newspapers like the

Bangabasi in Calcutta and the *Pioneer* and *Hasicher Patrika* in Punjab. Yet despite the Indians' education and social status, the British still ran India. A few Englishmen ruled 350 million Indians. As the nineteenth century neared its close, the Indian elite grew impatient to be rid of the colonial masters.

The Indian National Congress

In December 1885, a group of about seventy wealthy men gathered in Bombay. They founded the Indian National Congress, the organization that would lead the way to an independent and democratic India. The congress became the voice of the independence movement. Its influence would be felt for many decades. An offshoot of the congress, the Congress party, survives in India today.

The creation of the Indian National Congress marked the formal start of India's struggle for independence from Great Britain. Many prominent Hindu and Muslim men joined the organization. At that time, Indian women were rarely educated or members of the workforce. Yet a few women did participate in the congress. With Gandhi's support, women, including his wife, Kasturbhai, contributed to the nationalist movement. Congress members published editorials in Indian newspapers and held public rallies. Some four hundred fifty members attended its second meeting. Many thousands more cheered at demonstrations in villages across the country.

At first, the British cautiously supported the Indian National Congress. Three British men served as president of the congress between 1885 and 1890. In its early years, the congress set modest goals for limited democratic reforms under British rule.

Swaraj

By the start of the twentieth century, the Indian National Congress had gained a strong foothold among the English-speaking middle class. At the same time, the industrialization of India was under way. Industry offered the promise that, one day, India could join the world economy without relying on Great Britain's support. In 1905, the congress began calling for *swaraj*, the Sanskrit word for self-rule, for India.

However, congress members did not always agree on the best way to achieve self-government. Would India's freedom be won through protests and demands, or through negotiation and compromise with the British? The Indians who worked for the government had to be careful if they wanted to keep their jobs. The lawyers and politicians, on the other hand, were more eager for independence at all costs.

Some in the congress, known as Moderates, believed independence could be achieved through gradual changes in the laws and government. The quiet, scholarly Gopal Krishna Gokhale was a leader of the Moderates. Like many Indians, Gokhale admired the British traditions of discipline, duty, organization, and loyalty.[2] Yet he knew that India could gain true self-respect only with independence. He also encouraged friendship between Hindus and Muslims, whose historic differences were deepening.

Gandhi first met Gokhale on a visit home to India from South Africa in 1896. Gokhale traveled to South Africa in 1912 to learn more about the civil rights struggle Gandhi was leading. Three years older than Gandhi, Gokhale became a friend and mentor to the younger man. After Gandhi returned to India, Gokhale helped him join the independence movement. But Gokhale's gentle voice of reason and reconciliation was silenced when he died in 1915, shortly after Gandhi's return.

Other independence leaders were more impatient. Bal Gangadhar Tilak, a lawyer and mathematician, was the fiery leader of the Extremists. The Extremists believed in a national identity for India and Hinduism as a national religion. They were prepared to take action and rise up against the British, rather than negotiate. Tilak wore a bright red turban and led public protests. He was arrested for sedition, or inciting people to revolt against the government, in 1908. He was jailed for six years.

After Tilak was released in 1914, the moderate voice grew fainter. India was no longer willing to wait for its freedom. Although the nationalists in the congress still debated among themselves, they would have to unite to defeat the British Raj.

British India

The British government was an organized, wealthy, and formidable opponent. British India consisted of eleven provinces ruled by local British governors, who were appointed by the British monarch. The governors reported to the British viceroy, the head of the Indian government, who was also appointed by the monarch. A separate secretary of state in London served in the British Cabinet. The viceroy was the most powerful person in India. Some viceroys were more popular and sympathetic to the Indians than others. The British Raj was centered in Calcutta, until the capital was moved to Delhi in 1911.

The Indian Civil Service

The job of managing British India was left to an elite group of about a thousand British men in the Indian Civil Service, the massive government bureaucracy. They were trained in Indian languages and culture in special courses at prestigious universities. The British in India also included indigo and tea planters, entrepreneurs, railroad employees, and missionaries.

The British hired Indian servants, who called their employers *sahibs* and *memsahibs*, the Urdu words for master and mistress, respectively. Some Indians worked as policemen and low-level government bureaucrats. But most Indians had little personal contact with the British. Many had never even seen a European. The British lived apart from the Indians in self-contained compounds. They played British sports, worshiped at their own churches, buried their dead in their own graveyards, and socialized at their own clubs.

Hunting tigers and other large game animals was a popular sport among the men. In the summer, British officials and their families moved to Simla in the foothills of the Himalayas and other high-altitude places, known as hill stations. There, they socialized in British tea houses, dining on traditional English food. As one writer observed, the British tried to "re-create England in India."[3]

Though the British often became ill from the extreme climate, unfamiliar food, and unsanitary water, some developed a passionate interest in India. The British government sent photographers to record India's people and landscape. Still, a deep gap remained between the two cultures.

After Indian soldiers rebelled against the British in the Sepoy Rebellion in 1857, relations deteriorated. The Victorian Era, from 1837 to 1901, brought with it a sense of moral superiority among the British. By the 1870s, Great Britain was the richest country in the world. With this prosperity came a renewed zeal to convert the world to Christianity. "The vast majority of Indians were Hindus and, therefore, pagans in need of conversion," wrote historian Lawrence James.[4] British and Indian intermarriage was not accepted by either culture.

The British were often perplexed by India's religions and customs. At the same time, Indians felt the British were arrogant and racist. Many writers described life in British India. British writer E. M. Forster's 1924 classic, *A Passage to India*, criticized colonial rule while telling the story of tragic misunderstandings between British civil servants and the Indian middle class. Rudyard Kipling, a British writer born in Bombay in 1865, wrote dozens of short stories and books supporting British colonialism. He believed the British had a moral duty to civilize the untamed Indian. His classic tale, *Kim*, tells of an orphaned white boy in British India who travels with an old Buddhist holy man in search of his identity. For a time, Kim attends British boarding school with the sons of British colonialists, absorbing their sense of superiority over Indians. "One must never forget that one is a Sahib [European master], and that some day, when examinations are passed, one will command natives. Kim made a note of this," wrote Kipling.[5]

British Railroads and Schools

In fact, India gained many benefits from British rule. In the 1850s, British engineers and Indian laborers built the first Indian railroad to transport cotton to Bombay for shipment to the English mills. The railroad also moved the Anglo-Indian Army. India's railroad system would become one of the world's largest. The British also brought modern postal, telegraph, and telephone systems to India. British irrigation systems helped reduce the frequent drought-induced famines. British educators built

Indian workers build the Indian railroad, one of the technological improvements brought by the British. However, the rule of the British brought more hardship than help for native Indians.

schools and colleges, though never a public education system. The introduction of the English language allowed India to communicate with the rest of the world.

Yet most advancements added profits to Great Britain's treasury without helping ordinary Indians. Indian taxpayers paid for the railroad, which opened new markets and transported goods for British trade. The poor went into debt to pay high taxes to landlords who lived in England. Indian soldiers fought and died for the British in wars. Despite improvements in irrigation and living conditions for some Indians, a succession of famines killed, by one estimate, 18 million Indians during the nineteenth century. Meanwhile, the British Raj prospered.[6]

The Partition of Bengal and Growing Unrest

A terrorist movement, fueled by religious hatred between Hindus and Muslims, swept through India in the early 1900s. Lord George Nathaniel Curzon, the viceroy at the time, was an imperialist, or a strong supporter of the British Empire. He believed Great Britain should protect India's cultural history and prepare Indians for the future.

In 1905, he made the controversial decision to partition, or divide, Bengal, a heavily populated state in northeast India. Torn by religious unrest, Bengal was difficult to govern. The partition of Bengal into separate Hindu and Muslim states sparked protests, shootings, and bombings by both groups.

Fearing more violence, the British government passed the Morley-Minto Reforms of 1909. For the first time, a small number of Indians was elected to the viceroy's executive council and the provincial legislative councils. These important governing councils would, thereafter, no longer be dominated by senior British civil servants.

In 1911, the new British king, George V, and Queen Mary were honored in a great ceremony, or *durbar*, in Delhi, the new Indian capital. George V was the only British monarch to visit India during the colonial era. In another gesture designed to quiet India's discontent, the British announced the reversal of the Bengal partition.

The Muslim League

The events in Bengal showed the growing tension between Hindus and Muslims throughout India. Hindus and Muslims had been uneasy neighbors at least since the Mughal period, when a small number of Muslims dominated a Hindu majority. The mutual dislike was based not so much on religious intolerance as on social division. With the end of the Mughal Empire, Muslims felt excluded from full participation in India's mostly Hindu society. Although some Muslims joined the Indian National Congress, many feared what would happen to them if Great Britain left India.

In 1906, a group of prosperous Muslims formed a separate political organization, the Muslim League, with the support of the British government. Muslims were well represented in the police and army, and many were loyal to the British. However, they also wanted India's freedom. By supporting the Muslims, some scholars believe the British deliberately tried to divide India and weaken the nationalist movement. "Divide and rule" by religion and region had always been a tenet of colonial policy.

Mohammed Ali Jinnah was the president of the Muslim League.

The best known Muslim in the nationalist movement was Mohammed Ali Jinnah. He was a slender, articulate lawyer from a wealthy family. His grandfather was a Hindu. A good friend of Gandhi's for many years, Jinnah at first favored a Hindu and Muslim alliance. But he grew suspicious of the Hindu nationalists. As president of the Muslim League, Jinnah would play a decisive role as the division between Hindu and Muslim shaped India's future.

India was in turmoil when Gandhi returned from South Africa in 1915. There was growing resentment against colonial authority. The distrust between Hindus and Muslims had grown deeper. India had changed since Gandhi had sailed to South Africa as a young man. Gandhi had changed as well.

Chapter 6

Rebellion and Reform

Thousands of people crowded the wharves to welcome Gandhi and his family when the S.S. *Arabia* dropped anchor in Bombay Harbor in January 1915. Word of Gandhi's work on behalf of human rights for Indians in South Africa had spread through India. Gandhi was a national hero.

Gandhi was returning to India after nearly twenty-two years. Unsure of what his future held, he felt like a stranger in his own country. He had spent the previous five months in London, organizing an Indian ambulance corps for the British war effort in World War I. When that work was done, Gandhi did not know what to do next. The only answer was to go home.

Determined to learn more about his own country, Gandhi spent a year touring the villages and cities of India. He visited Bengal, Burma, Delhi, Madras, and his home state of Gujarat. "He insisted on traveling third class by train, and was appalled by the curt way the poor were treated by railway officials," wrote biographer Judith Brown.[1] When he visited Hardwar, the holy city on the Ganges River, India's holiest river, he was shocked at the people's poverty and the lack of sanitation. Indians in their own country suffered the same problems as the Indians in South Africa: a lack of human rights and dignity. Gandhi had found his purpose.

The Indigo Rebellion

Soon, Gandhi undertook his first project in India. For many generations, farmers in the remote region of Champaran in Bihar had worked the fields of indigo. The plant's natural blue dye was a valuable export for British India, but not for the Indian people. The large Bihar indigo farms were run by British planters and worked by Indian sharecroppers, people who farmed land they did not own. The tenants planted indigo and used their harvests to pay rent to the owners of the land. They barely earned enough to feed themselves. The profitable British-owned indigo factories made the plants into dye.

After Germany developed synthetic indigo in the early 1900s, the British no longer needed the indigo crops. So the sharecroppers were forced to pay higher rents and fees to be released from their indigo contracts. When indigo prices soared during World War I because German synthetic indigo was in short supply, the British insisted that the land again be planted with indigo. At the mercy of the landowners, the Indians were desperate to reform this system.

One farmer named Rajkumar Shukla attended the Indian National Congress meeting at Lucknow in December 1916. He was there to tell the story of the indigo workers. No one paid attention—until he spoke with Gandhi. Gandhi was reluctant to become involved, but Shukla insisted that Gandhi visit Champaran and see the situation for himself.

Gandhi agreed to travel to Champaran and investigate. There, he spoke with farmers and collected information about the indigo industry. Soon British officials began to suspect that Gandhi was a troublemaker. They ordered him to leave. Gandhi refused. If necessary, he was willing to go to jail. "I feel it to be my duty to say that I am unable to leave this District but if it so pleases the authorities, I shall submit to the order by suffering the penalty of disobedience," he wrote to the officials.[2]

Gandhi was put on trial for disregarding the order to leave. The courts in colonial India were run by the British. British men served as judges and prosecutors. Thousands of people smashed the glass doors during Gandhi's trial, trying to push their way into the courtroom. The judge feared riots would occur if Gandhi were imprisoned. He dismissed the case and apologized to Gandhi. Gandhi continued gathering information about the situation in Champaran. Fearing an uprising, the government did not dare arrest him.

In May 1917, Gandhi presented his report to the British authorities. He and his assistants had documented low wages, illegal fines, unfair land distribution, and a labor system in which the farmers were virtually slaves. As a result of Gandhi's report, the planters agreed to pay back some of the money they had taken from the tenants and to establish fairer working conditions. "In Champaran I declared that the British could not order me about in my own country," Gandhi said later.[3] There was no doubt that the British had an effective opponent. "He had won his first battle on Indian soil," wrote biographer Robert Payne.[4]

More Battles on Behalf of the Poor

The Indian National Congress grew more demanding during these years. In 1916, the Extremist leader, Tilak, founded the Home Rule League with Annie Besant, a British woman who had joined the Indian nationalists. Together with the congress, the Home Rule League called for democratic reforms and swift independence.

Gandhi joined the Indian National Congress in 1917. He soon became its leader. Under Gandhi's direction, the congress, once a small group of educated professionals, reached out across religious and caste lines to become a campaign of the masses. The congress became a real political party, with the support of millions of ordinary Indians in rural villages and cities.

Gandhi soon took up more battles on behalf of India's peasants. In 1918, Gandhi supported a strike of textile workers against mill owners in Ahmedabad. It was there that he discovered the power of a hunger strike. The workers had requested a 35 percent wage increase. The mill owners offered only 20 percent. Ten thousand workers walked off their jobs. Frustrated at the lack of agreement between the two sides, Gandhi began a hunger strike in protest. After he had fasted for three days, the mill owners agreed to the 35 percent increase.

One of the strike leaders, Vallabhbhai Patel, a lawyer and the son of a poor farmer, became a close friend of Gandhi's. Patel would also become an important organizer for the Indian National Congress.

The Rowlatt Acts

Hoping to control the rising dissent, the British announced the Royal Proclamation of 1917. It provided for the gradual self-government of India. Still, nationalists felt it did not go far enough.

World War I ended in November 1918. Nearly a hundred thousand Indian soldiers had died fighting for the British Empire. Indians expected that their loyalty to Great Britain would be rewarded. But they were disappointed. Soldiers returned home to find themselves still under Great Britain's rule.

To combat the antigovernment protests going on across India, the British government passed the Rowlatt Acts in March 1919. The laws suspended civil rights and instituted martial law, or the suspension of civil liberties, in places where people were rioting. Terrorism was outlawed. So were acts of resistance against the government. The law also authorized imprisonment without trial.

Outraged, Gandhi organized a *hartal*, or a general strike. The people of India would fast, and all government business and trade would cease for one day on April 6, 1919. Gandhi hoped the hartal would force the government to suspend the Rowlatt Acts.

But even before the strike began, violence broke out in Delhi. On March 30, riots and parades of Indians protesting British rule brought out British troops. British soldiers shot and killed five Hindus and four Muslims. Even so, on April 6, Gandhi led a peaceful one-day strike in Bombay.

Soon after, Gandhi was briefly arrested on the train from Bombay to Delhi. He was released, but not before news of his arrest led to rioting across India. Protesters cut telegraph wires and tore up railroad tracks. Some Europeans were killed. Gandhi quickly called off the hartal. This would not be the last time that Gandhi's call for nonviolent protest resulted in bloodshed.

Amritsar Massacre

Worse was yet to come. The city of Amritsar was in turmoil. British officials had arrested two leading nationalists, Saifuddin Kitchlew and Satya Pal. Indian crowds attacked Europeans and their property. On April 13, 1919, thousands of unarmed Indians gathered in Jallianwala alla Bagh, an enclosed area surrounded by walls. Some historians say the gathering was a religious celebration. Others describe it as a mass meeting against the British.

Whatever its purpose, any large gathering defied a British order banning all public meetings. British Brigadier General Reginald Dyer led his Indian troops to break up the crowds. Without warning, the soldiers fired on the defenseless people. They killed nearly four hundred and left more than twelve hundred wounded. Two days after the massacre, martial law was declared. The British condemned the

Source Document

If India takes up the doctrine of the sword, she may gain momentary victory, but then India will cease to be the pride of my heart.[5]

Gandhi made this statement to nationalists who were demanding open rebellion against British rule after the Amritsar Massacre.

incident. General Dyer was relieved of his command. Even so, the Rowlatt Acts and the Amritsar Massacre proved to Indians that Great Britain was more concerned about putting down rebellion than granting freedom to India.

Gandhi Pleads for Nonviolence

Gandhi was devastated by the massacre. Still, he urged Indians not to unleash their anger. "Nothing but organized nonviolence can check the organized violence of the British government. . . . This nonviolence will be expressed through civil disobedience . . . ," he would write to the British viceroy in 1930.[6]

Poor farmers and professionals, Hindus and Muslims, and even many British began to look at Gandhi as a moral and spiritual leader. He did not want just freedom for India. He wanted to transform India with love and compassion for all its people, including the British. His political beliefs reflected his religious beliefs. These combined Hinduism, Christianity, Buddhism, and other religions. "[T]hose who say that religion has nothing to do with politics do not know what religion means," he once wrote.[7] The Bengali poet Rabindranath Tagore called Gandhi "The Great Soul in peasant's garb." Gandhi became known to millions as the *Mahatma*, the Sanskrit word meaning Great Soul. He did not like the title.

The Khilafat Movement

In the early 1920s, India's Muslims and Hindus formed a brief alliance, brought on by events outside

India. During World War I, the Ottoman Empire joined the Germans to fight against Great Britain. The sultan of Turkey led the Ottoman Empire and was also the spiritual head, or *caliph*, of all Muslims in the world. Thus, India's Muslims felt compelled to support Turkey's war efforts. After the Ottoman Empire collapsed at the end of World War I, Muslims tried to ensure that the sultan would survive as the Islamic leader. This became known as the Khilafat Movement.

In 1916, the Indian National Congress and the Muslims signed the Lucknow Pact. The pact offered Hindu support of the Khilafat Movement. It also guaranteed that Muslims would have special elections and reserved seats in the provincial and all-India government councils. In exchange, the Muslims agreed to join the nationalists in pressuring the British Raj to let India go. But the partnership was brief. When the modern secular Republic of Turkey was founded in 1923, the sultan lost his position. Muslim fears of Hindu domination in India returned. The alliance then broke down.

Noncooperation

In August 1920, at Gandhi's urging, the Indian National Congress launched a noncooperation movement to boycott the British government. Noncooperation meant refusing to pay taxes or buy British goods. Gandhi advised Indians to take their children out of British schools and colleges. He asked them to give up their British titles. Gandhi returned the British medal he had received for organizing Indian ambulance corps in South Africa.

Despite Gandhi's insistence on nonviolence, his remarks continued to fuel riots. When the Prince of Wales, the future King Edward VIII, arrived in Bombay in November 1921, the Indian National Congress organized a general strike to boycott his visit. Mob violence erupted when some crowds, going against the congress's wishes, turned out to welcome the prince. Protesters looted shops and burned foreign cloth. They set cars on fire. Policemen were killed. Gandhi saw the street violence for himself when he drove through Bombay. He tried in vain to stop the riots. But the situation would only get worse.

On February 5, 1922, a group of nationalist protesters was marching past a police station in the small village of Chauri Chaura. Police began taunting them. Fighting broke out, and the police opened fire. When they ran out of ammunition, the police barricaded themselves inside the station. The mob set the building on fire, forcing the police to flee into the angry crowd. Twenty-two policemen were killed.

Gandhi Is Jailed

Gandhi blamed himself for the violence. He began a fast to relieve his sense of guilt. Fearing more upheaval, he called off the noncooperation campaign. But the British viceroy, Lord Rufus Isaacs Reading, decided that the time had come to arrest Gandhi for trying to overthrow the government with his writings and speeches. Hundreds of congress followers had already been jailed.

On the evening of March 10, the superintendent of police at Ahmedabad drove to the ashram at Sabarmati to place Gandhi under arrest. Gandhi gathered up a spare loincloth, blankets, and books, then walked to the police car. At his trial on March 18, 1922, Gandhi pled guilty to the charges of sedition. He said:

> I want to avoid violence. . . . But I had to make my choice. I had either to submit to a system which I considered had done irreparable harm to my country, or incur the risk of the mad fury of my people bursting forth, when they understood the truth from my lips . . .[8]

He requested the most severe penalty—six years in prison.

Gandhi spent four years in his cell at the Yeravda jail. He stayed busy reading, writing his autobiography, and spinning cotton yarn. Gandhi was released in 1924, after he developed acute appendicitis and needed an operation.

Steps Toward Self-government

Gandhi's noncooperation movement of the early 1920s did not bring down the British Raj. However, in the midst of the riots and bloodshed, Anglo-Indian relations began to change slowly. In 1917, the new secretary of state for India, Edwin Montagu, came to India. His job was to look for ways to stabilize the Raj and satisfy middle-class nationalists. Montagu felt that Great Britain needed to rely less on force and more on India's cooperation. He decided that the goal of British policy should be "increasing association of Indians in every branch of the administration, and the gradual development of self-governing institutions, with a view to the progressive realizing of responsible government in India as an integral part of the British Empire."[9]

With the viceroy, Lord John Napier Chelmsford, Montagu developed reforms to give Indians more participation in government. The Montagu-Chelmsford proposals, known as the Montford Reforms, created two levels of government elected by Indian voters. There would be provincial assemblies, with Indian ministers in charge of education, health, agriculture, and the state budget. A national legislative assembly would have an advisory role. Men who owned property and officers of the Indian Army were given the vote.

The reforms, put in place in the early 1920s, gave more authority to the provinces. Before this, the provinces had little say about finance and laws. Now the provinces could collect certain taxes and decide how to spend the money. The provincial governments could also pass some of their own laws. The central British-run government would remain in charge of defense, foreign affairs, commerce, and other national matters. The viceroy and the British provincial governors would control the police. They could veto any new laws.

The Empire Weakens

Meanwhile, World War I had left Great Britain exhausted. The British Empire had become too expensive to govern. During the 1920s and 1930s, Great Britain would look for ways to reduce the empire's cost.

The colonies were also restless. Egypt revolted against colonial rule and won its independence in 1922. In 1931, the empire was reorganized into the British Commonwealth of Nations. The commonwealth is an association of equal and independent states united by allegiance to the British Crown. However, Great Britain retained control of Egypt's monarchy until 1953.

This turbulent time of protests and reforms shaped the next phase of India's freedom struggle. The nationalists learned that they could stand up to the British. In turn, the British realized that the Indian National Congress, led by Gandhi, was a "formidable force" in a discontented nation.[10]

Chapter 7

The Spinning Wheel and Nehru

In many ways, Gandhi was an unlikely leader for one of history's greatest freedom movements. He was a private, spiritual man, who struggled throughout his life with religious questions and moral doubts. Gandhi was always striving to improve himself and to find answers to life's most basic questions. "Turn the searchlight inward," he often said.[1]

Soon after Gandhi returned to India in 1915, he and his wife, Kasturbhai, founded the Satyagraha Ashram. It was located at Kochrab near Ahmedabad, a textile center in central India not far from Gandhi's birthplace. Two years later, he moved the ashram to the banks of the Sabarmati River. The community contained a library, a school, kitchens, houses, and cotton fields. As in South Africa, the ashram was a refuge where Gandhi lived quietly between his travels.

In these peaceful surroundings, Gandhi—the lawyer, philosopher, and rebel—began spinning cotton yarn.

India's Cotton Wealth

For centuries, cotton spinning and weaving had been India's most important home industry. Indian cotton was worn all over Africa and Asia. After the 1850s, the British textile mills turned to India as a source for raw cotton. Now India had to send its cotton to England's mills, rather than use the cotton to make goods at home. Indians were forced to buy manufactured goods, including cloth, from England. Those who had spun cotton and sewn cloth in their homes and villages were thrown out of work.

Without jobs, these laborers turned to farming. Famine increased as India's millions of poor farmers struggled to survive. The import of textiles and clothing from the British mills of Lancashire and Manchester had destroyed the livelihoods of India's home weavers. Great Britain also built mills in India. With the spinning wheel as his weapon, Gandhi took a stand against British imports.

The Spinning Wheel

Gandhi found an old *charkha*, or spinning wheel, and set it up in his study. He invited a handspinning expert to teach ashram members how to spin yarn. "The object that we set before ourselves was to be able to clothe ourselves entirely in cloth manufactured by our own hands," he wrote.[2] The ashram members promised to wear handwoven cloth made only from

Gandhi took up spinning yarn to promote a return to the traditional industries and lifestyles of India. He is seen here spinning in 1947.

Indian yarn. Gandhi worked at the spinning wheel for hours every day.

Khadi—homespun cloth— became a symbol of Gandhi's determination to set India free from British rule. The campaign to wear cloth made only in India was known as the Swadeshi Movement. *Swadeshi* is a Bengali word meaning belonging to one's own country. By 1921, Gandhi had decided to wear only a *dhoti*—a loose loincloth made of homespun cotton—and sandals. Often he wore no shirt, just a cotton shawl. Even in formal meetings with British officials, he was often barefoot and bare chested. By dressing like the poorest Indian, he showed his belief in a simple life, his connection with the poor, and his protest against British imperialism.

Many Indian National Congress members adopted the uniform of dhotis, cotton shawls, and simple "Gandhi" hats of homespun cotton. The plain round cloth hats fit snugly on their heads. This uniform made congress members stand out as a mass movement. During the noncooperation protests of the early 1930s, Gandhi urged Indians to throw away or burn clothes made of foreign cloth and to boycott stores that sold foreign clothing.

Gandhi held huge bonfires in Bombay and other cities. In the novel *Swami and Friends* by Indian author R. K. Narayan, ten-year-old Swaminathan, a middle-class Indian boy, studies English and European history in school and plays the British game of cricket with his friends. But one day he finds himself caught up in a street demonstration against foreign clothing:

> Somebody asked him: "Young man, do you want our country to remain in eternal slavery?"
>
> "No, no," Swaminathan replied.
>
> "But you are wearing a foreign cap."
>
> Swaminathan quailed with shame. "Oh, I didn't notice," he said, and removing his cap flung it into the fire with a feeling that he was saving the country.[3]

The boycott worked. British textile companies lost a good deal of business in India.

A Return to Traditions

The Indian National Congress supported Gandhi's Swadeshi Movement. The nationalists also called for boycotts of British goods to break the colonial ties. However, Gandhi wanted to go a step farther. He hoped to build a new Indian society based on India's traditional village lifestyle of family, work, and religion. He disliked science and technology. He felt they ignored the individual. Modern machinery was evil, Gandhi believed, because it put wealth into the hands of the factory owners, not the people who did the labor. "Today machinery merely helps a few to ride on the back of millions," wrote Gandhi.[4]

Gandhi felt that the heart of India was its thousands of small villages. He wanted to revive village life by promoting literacy, improving sanitation, providing basic medical care, and improving farming techniques. He urged Indians to return to traditional handicrafts such as carpetmaking, spinning, weaving, and dyeing. He urged his fellow congress members to go to the villages and teach the people to read and to practice better sanitation.

Rifts in His Family

Sometimes, Gandhi's strong convictions caused problems within his own family. For example, to show his sympathy with India's poorest and most deprived, he invited an untouchable couple, Gangabehn and Ramjibhai Badhia, to live at the ashram, despite the

Source Document

The Real India lies in the 700,000 villages. If Indian civilization is to make its full contribution to the building up of a stable world order, it is this vast mass of humanity that has . . . to be made to live again.[5]

Gandhi spoke about the return of village industries and the need for improvement in living standards in India's villages.

objections of Kasturbhai and others. Ramjibhai was an expert weaver.

Gandhi also disapproved of teaching the English language, Western history, and science to Indian children. He did not want his sons enrolled in British schools. As a result, his sons were poorly educated. Harilal, his eldest son, especially resented Gandhi's decision about his education. Gandhi and Harilal grew apart. They barely spoke for the rest of their lives. Although Harilal joined Gandhi in the Indian civil rights struggle in South Africa, he was not involved in the Satyagraha movement in India. Harilal chose to convert to Islam, despite Gandhi's disapproval. As an adult, he rarely saw his father.

Critics

Many modern scholars question Gandhi's desire to turn his back on technology and revive the simple lifestyle and traditional handicrafts of India. *New York Times* reporter John F. Burns wrote in 1998:

> Many in the post-independence era have found his ascetic [abstaining from the normal pleasures of life] insistence on self-reliance and self-denial too demanding, and too otherworldly, to have much relevance in the India he bequeathed [handed down or passed on]. . . .[6]

Among the skeptics during Gandhi's own lifetime was his good friend and fellow nationalist Jawaharlal Nehru.

Gandhi (right) and Jawaharlal Nehru (left), despite the differences in their ages and ideas about the best way to free India from British rule, became friends and partners in the struggle for an independent India.

Nehru

Jawaharlal Nehru was the eldest son of Motilal Nehru, one of India's most respected lawyers. Motilal was a dedicated nationalist who was active in the Indian National Congress. He died in 1930 after being jailed for participating in the civil disobedience movement.

Jawaharlal Nehru, born in 1889, came from a world very different from Gandhi's. He grew up in privilege and luxury. His family's elegant home had a swimming pool and tennis courts. Educated at the elite Harrow School and the University of Cambridge in England, he almost did not return to India. He enjoyed life in England and travels in Europe. "The two men could not have been a greater contrast," wrote Gandhi biographer Judith M. Brown.[7] Yet Nehru shared with Gandhi a deep love of India.

Nehru was gifted with a brilliant mind and a way with words. Returning to India in 1912 to practice law, Nehru joined the Indian National Congress in 1919. He soon became Gandhi's protégé and a nationalist leader in his own right. He was popular with the Indian people. They called him *Pandit*, or "learned one." He always wore one rose in the buttonhole of his cotton vest. Yet, despite his charm and elegance, Nehru was moody. He often preferred to be alone.

Nehru deeply admired Gandhi. They agreed on many ideas about India's fight for independence. But Nehru was not religious. Nor did he share Gandhi's conviction that self-denial, abstinence (strict diet and celibacy), and spinning cotton were the paths to a new India. Nehru was skeptical of the effectiveness of peaceful resistance. "A vast distance seemed to separate him [Gandhi] from me," Nehru wrote.[8]

Like Gandhi, Nehru wanted to preserve India's culture. However, he also believed that India needed technology to bring it into the modern world. "In India especially, where we have been wedded far too long to past forms and modes of thought and action, new experiences, new processes, leading to new ideas and new horizons, are necessary," he observed.[9]

Chapter 8

Quit India

The Salt March of 1930 gave the nationalist movement a fresh burst of energy. During the next three years, the civil disobedience movement led by Gandhi swept across India. Gandhi became an international symbol of India's freedom struggle. The British tried, but failed, to stop the rebellion by jailing the nationalists. Some sixty thousand Indian protesters were jailed in the early 1930s for defying the Raj.

Fearing more riots and protests from Gandhi's followers, the viceroy, Lord Edward Wood Irwin, released Gandhi from prison just weeks after his arrest for leading the Salt March. Irwin invited Gandhi to Delhi to meet Winston Churchill, the British prime minister. Churchill was unimpressed with Gandhi, who carried his bamboo staff and wore his dhoti to the viceroy's house. Above all, Churchill was unwilling to agree to India's freedom. "The loss of India would be final and fatal to us," declared Churchill. He took a dislike to Gandhi, whom he described as a "half-naked" and "seditious fakir," an insult for a Hindu holy man.[1] His views did not change over the years.

Despite Churchill's attitude, Irwin and Gandhi negotiated the Gandhi-Irwin Pact on March 5, 1931. Irwin agreed to release thousands of Gandhi's followers from jail, if Gandhi ended the civil disobedience movement and attended a Round Table Conference in London to discuss India's future. Gandhi spent the autumn of 1931 in London. He made many friends among the British. But the negotiations were a failure. Gandhi could not convince British officials to free India. Great Britain was not ready to give up its favorite colony.

A week after he returned to India, Gandhi was back in Yeravda jail. A new viceroy, Lord Freeman Willingdon, and a more conservative government in London outlawed the Indian National Congress and arrested many congress leaders. Within four months, eighty thousand Indians were jailed. Still, progress had been made. "For the first time since the British took away India from the Indians, they had been forced . . . to deal with an Indian leader as an equal," wrote one historian.[2]

Fasting for the Harijans

In prison, Gandhi turned his attention to India's untouchables. Gandhi was dismayed at India's treatment of the casteless people. He called them *Harijans*, the "Children of God." In August 1932, Gandhi announced a fast until death if conditions for untouchables did not improve. He opposed a proposal by some Hindu leaders to give untouchables separate seats in provincial legislatures. Separating the untouchable vote would further divide India, Gandhi said, and make untouchability even more accepted. This was a controversial stance. Many untouchable leaders disagreed with their most famous advocate.

Gandhi's September fast was a success. The British agreed to change the law. The Hindu people responded, too. A few days after his last meal of lemon juice and honey, Hindu temple doors were opened to untouchables for the first time. Untouchables were allowed to take water from public wells and walk freely on public streets. But changing the attitudes of Hindus would take time. After a couple of weeks, the temple doors quietly closed again.

Source Document

I shall work for an India in which the poorest shall feel it is their country . . . an India in which all communities shall live in perfect harmony. . . . This is the India of my dreams.[3]

Gandhi wrote this statement during the Harijan movement in 1931.

Gandhi did not give up. When Gandhi was released from prison in 1933, after another fast, he began a twelve-thousand-mile pilgrimage through India. He hoped to convince caste Hindus to stop discriminating against untouchables. He walked for nine months, often jeered by Orthodox Hindus. At the end of the march, a bomb was thrown at him and his followers, leaving seven people injured. But Gandhi was undeterred. "The agony of soul is not going to end until every trace of untouchability is gone," Gandhi wrote.[4] For the rest of his life, Gandhi pushed for reforms to benefit India's untouchables.

The Salt March and other protests of the early 1930s resulted in concessions by the British. The Government of India Act of 1935 provided a framework for the future self-government of India. This important act granted voting rights to one sixth of the Indian population, both men and women who owned property. The provinces of India became self-governing. The stage was set for a national Indian government, if the maharajas agreed to join the provinces. But the maharajas were reluctant to give up their special status. Until they did, the British kept their central authority over India and control over defense and foreign policy. In the nationwide elections of April 1937, many congress members took office in provinces with Hindu majorities. But the viceroy had the last say. India remained under British rule.

World War II

Political developments in Europe soon overshadowed India's independence struggle. During the late 1930s, the rise in Germany of Adolf Hitler, founder of the National Socialist Workers' (Nazi) party, posed a threat to world peace. In September 1939, Great Britain declared war on Germany after Hitler invaded Poland. World War II had begun.

The following spring, Germany invaded Denmark, Norway, Holland, Belgium, and France. Italy's fascist government, a totalitarian regime led by Benito Mussolini that denied all individual liberties, joined Germany. By 1940, France had fallen to Germany. In December 1941, Japan, an ally of Germany and Italy, attacked Pearl Harbor in Hawaii, bringing the United States into the war.

In 1934, Gandhi retired from the Indian National Congress. He retreated to his ashram for meditation, fasting, and prayer. But he still traveled around India, preaching nonviolence and the fair treatment of untouchables. Gandhi handed the reins of the independence movement over to Jawaharlal Nehru. Nehru would be the one to negotiate with the British during the transition to independence. He, not Gandhi, would lead India into the modern age.

Gandhi kept up with political developments in congress, often consulting Indian leaders. Meanwhile, he founded a new ashram at Savagram at Wardha in central India. As a pacifist, he disapproved of the war and especially Hitler's aggression. Gandhi wrote an open letter to Hitler condemning war.

Great Britain had declared war against Germany on September 3, 1939. As part of the British Empire, India was expected to join Great Britain on the battlefield. The congress was outraged that the British government did not consult India before committing some three hundred thousand Indian troops to battle. Indian nationalists opposed fascism and Nazism for robbing people of their civil rights and liberties and putting power in the hands of dictators. But they could not support India's forced entry into the war. In protest, congress members resigned their posts in

Source Document

It is quite clear that you are today the one person in the world who can prevent a war which may reduce humanity to the savage state. Must you pay that price for an object however worthy it may appear to you to be? Will you listen to the appeal of one who has deliberately shunned the method of war not without considerable success?[5]

Gandhi wrote this letter to German dictator Adolf Hitler on July 23, 1939, just before World War II began.

provincial governments. They continued to press for independence.

India's shaken loyalty to Great Britain was further tested when Japanese armed forces neared India. By the early 1940s, Japan, opposing Great Britain and the Allies, occupied much of the British Empire in Southeast Asia, including Hong Kong, Singapore, and Sumatra. Indians feared that Japanese soldiers would soon cross the borders. With the nationalists fueling anti-British sentiment, Great Britain was unsure whether India would help fight the Japanese.

The Cripps Mission Fails

On March 22, 1942, Sir Stafford Cripps, a member of the British War Cabinet, arrived in New Delhi to meet with Indian leaders. He was a friend of Nehru's and supported Indian self-determination.

Cripps offered dominion status to India in return for help in fighting the Japanese. Dominion status would allow India to have limited self-government as a member of the British Commonwealth of Nations. Under the Cripps proposal, India could secede, or separate itself, from the commonwealth when the war ended. This would bring India closer to independence.

Gandhi feared that, after the war, the agreement would allow India to divide by religious and ethnic groups into many small countries. Nehru, on the other hand, felt it did not go far enough. In the end, both the Indian National Congress and Muslim League rejected Cripps's proposal.

Gandhi (left) greets Sir Stafford Cripps (right) in 1946.

Quit India

After the unsuccessful negotiations, the nationalist furor grew more intense. Gandhi was back in politics. He sent a resolution, which he called "Quit India," to the congress. In it, he demanded Great Britain's immediate withdrawal from India. The congress accepted the resolution.

Gandhi then began a campaign to force out the British. "Leave India to God, or in modern parlance [language], to anarchy," declared Gandhi. Speaking to his followers in Bombay in August 1942, Gandhi warned: "Do or die. We shall either free India or die in the attempt; we shall not live to see the perpetuation of our slavery."[6]

Gandhi's loyal assistant, Madeleine Slade, the daughter of an English admiral, asked to meet with the viceroy but was refused. She left him this message about Gandhi: "[N]o crushing force will silence him. The more you crush, the more his power will spread. You are faced with two alternatives; one to declare India's Independence, and the other to kill Gandhiji [an affectionate name for Gandhi]."[7]

Kasturbhai Is Gone

Great Britain could not tolerate antigovernment threats during wartime. The British arrested Gandhi, Slade, Nehru, and dozens of congress members on August 9. Gandhi's wife, Kasturbhai, was arrested, too, when she prepared to deliver a speech in Bombay that Gandhi was unable to give because he

Kasturbhai, seen here in a portrait taken in 1915, was Gandhi's wife and partner through many years of public work. Although she did not always agree with Gandhi's methods, she supported him in his efforts to free the people of India.

was then in jail. Violence spread through India. Anti-British protesters burned police stations. Railroad tracks were torn up. Telegraph lines were cut and British officials were murdered.

The British locked Gandhi in the Aga Kahn's palace at Poona, surrounded by a high barbed-wire fence. He was accompanied by Kasturbhai, who was terrified of prison. She was also in ill health from repeated heart attacks and bouts of pneumonia. Gandhi's longtime secretary and friend, Mahadev Desai, died suddenly of a heart attack while in prison with the Gandhis. Disturbed by his death, Kasturbhai grew weak. She was able to see her sons briefly, but the British guards did not make it easy. Gandhi refused to order penicillin for his wife. He often refused modern medical treatments for himself and his family. "If God wills it, He will pull her through," he said.[8] Kasturbhai died on February 22, 1944.

Gandhi and Kasturbhai had been married nearly sixty years. She had sometimes resented her husband's temper and stubbornness, but she had always remained at his side. Now Gandhi had lost his closest companion. Soon after her death, Gandhi fell ill with malaria, a mosquito-borne disease. On May 5, he was unexpectedly freed because of his ill health.

Muslim Riots and Civil War

World War II ended with an Allied victory in September 1945. Early in 1946, Great Britain offered India its independence as soon as Indian leaders could agree on a form of government. However, Hindus and Muslims were unable to resolve their differences.

The Muslim League had grown in power by the mid-1940s. Mohammed Jinnah became the leader of the Muslim League in 1935. Muslims worried that a free, democratic India would be dominated by the Hindu majority. In 1940, the league passed a resolution. It demanded an independent country for Muslims, a nation that would be called *Pakistan*, which means "land of the pure."

But Hindus did not want to give up land for a Muslim nation. Gandhi also did not want India to be divided. "Hindus and Muslims of India are not two nations. Those whom God has made one, man will never be able to divide," said Gandhi.[9]

The Muslim League called for a day of street demonstrations to show the desire for a new nation of Pakistan. On August 16, 1946, tens of thousands of

Muslims gathered in pro-Pakistan rallies in Calcutta in Bengal. Muslim rioting in Calcutta led to mass attacks on Hindus and their property. Hindus returned the violence. Within seventy-two hours, five thousand people lay dead in the streets.

Religious bloodshed spread across India. Over the next year, some twenty thousand people died in the uprisings. India was on the brink of civil war. Great Britain would have to act quickly.

Lord Mountbatten, the Last Viceroy

A great-grandson of Queen Victoria, Louis Francis Albert Victor Nicholas Mountbatten, Viscount of Burma, was called on to take the final steps to free India and begin dismantling the British Empire. The time had come. Great Britain was struggling to regain its economic footing after World War II. It could no longer afford to support its colonies. In addition, the liberal Labour government that had been elected in 1945, led by Prime Minister Clement Attlee, was sympathetic to nationalist causes. The Labour government was more concerned about getting rid of poverty and unemployment in England than supporting colonies abroad. It did not favor the colonial system.

A decorated naval officer, Mountbatten had served as Supreme Commander of the Allied Forces in Southeast Asia in World War II. Before leaving England, he was instructed by Attlee to negotiate with Gandhi, Nehru, and Jinnah for Indian independence within a year.

Source Document

I want you to regard me not as the last Viceroy winding up the British Raj but as the first to lead the way to the new India.[10]

Lord Mountbatten's statement upon his arrival in New Delhi.

On March 22, 1947, Lord Mountbatten and his wife, Lady Edwina Mountbatten, arrived in India. Ambitious, flamboyant, and liberal, Mountbatten was eager to win India's approval and friendship. "I am under no illusion about the difficulty of my task. . . . I shall need the greatest good will of the greatest possible number, and I am asking India today for that good will," he told Indian leaders at a welcoming ceremony shortly after arriving in Delhi. Mountbatten wore his admiral's dress whites and gleaming war medals. "Mountbatten looked more king than viceroy," wrote one observer.[11]

Nehru, now the leader of India's independence movement, was impressed by the viceroy, but mutual trust would take time. He did not want India to be forced into a future that was not in its best interest.

Gandhi met Lord Mountbatten shortly after Mountbatten's arrival. The two quickly became friends. Gandhi discovered that, although Mountbatten was a wealthy aristocrat and career soldier, he shared Gandhi's moral values. Unfortunately, Mountbatten never won the confidence of the Muslims. Muslim League leader Jinnah suspected the British diplomat was too close to the Hindus, and refused to negotiate with him. "The Muslim League will not yield an inch in its demand for Pakistan,"

Gandhi (left) is seen here with Lord Mountbatten at Viceroy House in Delhi in 1946. Despite their diverse backgrounds, the two men had a friendly relationship.

Jinnah declared.[12] India would either be divided or destroyed, Jinnah warned.

Nehru and Mountbatten reluctantly agreed that the only way to avoid civil war was to divide India into two nations, Hindu India and Muslim Pakistan. In June 1947, Mountbatten announced that the British government accepted the idea of partition. The Indian National Congress, the Muslim League, and the Sikhs—the religious minority who made up a large population in the Punjab—also approved the plan.

Gandhi was strongly opposed to dividing India. Indeed, the story of partition would be a bloody one. Many people would later wonder whether it had been the right choice.

Chapter 9

A New Nation
and the Death
of Gandhi

$\mathbf{O}$n August 15, 1947, tens of thousands of people
thronged the streets of New Delhi, the capital of the
new India. "People came on donkeys, on horseback
and on bicycles, walking and running, country people
with turbans of every shape and color imaginable,
their women in bright, festive saris [traditional Indian
women's dress] . . ." recounted one witness.[1] Hindu
temples and Muslim mosques were lit with strings of
electric bulbs. The sidewalks were noisy as people sang
the new Indian national anthem, *"Jana-Gana-Mana,"*
or "Thou Art the Ruler of the Minds of All People."
In a grand procession, flanked by guards on horses
and buglers, Mountbatten, Nehru, and other congress
leaders drove along, waving to jubilant crowds.
Gandhi was nowhere to be seen.

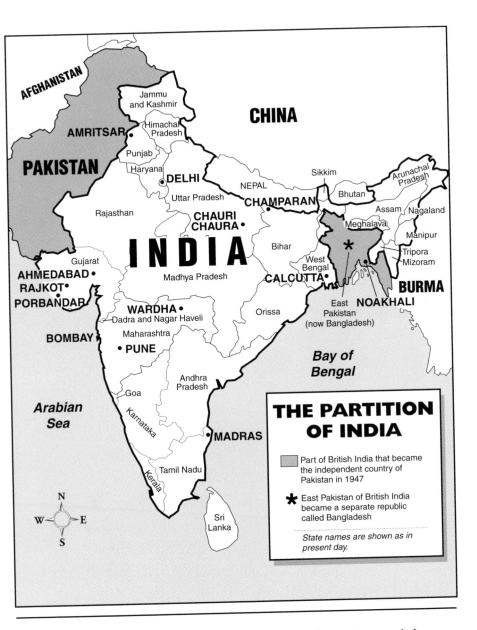

When Great Britain granted India its independence, it carved the new nation of Pakistan out of Indian soil to try to smooth the transition to independence among different religious groups.

The 400 million people of India were finally freed from British colonial rule. As the clock struck midnight on August 15, Nehru spoke on All-India Radio. "Long years ago we made a tryst [agreement or arrangement] with destiny, and now the time comes when we shall redeem our pledge, not wholly or in full measure, but very substantially," said Nehru.

> At the stroke of midnight hour, when the world sleeps, India will awake to life and freedom. A moment comes, which comes but rarely in history, when we step out from the old to the new, when an age ends, and when the soul of a nation, long suppressed, finds utterance.[2]

To set itself apart from India, Pakistan turned its clocks back thirty minutes in order to mark its independence on August 14.

For Nehru, the moment was bittersweet. He had spent nine years in British prisons for his outspoken support of India's self-determination. Nehru's joy that day was tempered by the religious violence that threatened to destroy the new nation. As he spoke, in Lahore in the Punjab, a hundred thousand Hindus and Sikhs were trapped inside the old walled city by Muslim mobs, who had set fire to Sikh and Hindu temples. Nevertheless, at five o'clock on August 15, India's new flag was raised at New Delhi's India Gate. The flag had the same colors as the Indian National Congress: saffron for courage and sacrifice, green for faith and fertility, and white for truth. The three colors also symbolize Hinduism, Islam, and India's many

Lord Mountbatten is seen here (at center, in white uniform) handing over power to Mohammed Ali Jinnah on August 14, 1947, the day Pakistan came into being.

other faiths. At its center is the Buddhist *dharma chakra*, or wheel of life.

With India's independence, the unraveling of the British Empire began. Great Britain soon granted independence to its colonies by transferring power to mostly friendly regimes. "Within the next decade, Britain's Far-Eastern and African empire had been dismantled with little heartache," observed one historian.[3] In 1997, Great Britain returned Hong Kong to China, leaving the British with no major colonial outposts. However, the British Commonwealth of

Nations, with the British monarch as its symbolic head, survives. Today, fifty-four independent nations, with 1.7 billion people, belong to the commonwealth. India is one of them.

Gandhi's Absence

The man who would be called the Father of India did not join in the celebrations of independence. "At this historic moment, let us not forget all that India owes to Mahatma Gandhi—the architect of her freedom through nonviolence. We miss his presence here today," said Lord Mountbatten.[4]

Far from the parades and speeches, Gandhi was fasting in an abandoned house in Calcutta. He had heard disturbing reports of massacres in the Punjab and riots in the state of Bihar. He was saddened that religious hatred was shattering his dream of a unified, free India.

At the request of Muslims, Gandhi spent much of 1946 and 1947 trying to stop the turbulence in Bihar and Bengal. In October 1946, he walked miles through Noakhali in East Bengal. He hoped to stop the massacres of Hindus by Muslims. The riots in Bihar particularly bothered Gandhi. This was where Gandhi had begun the Satyagraha movement for the indigo workers more than thirty years earlier. "If even half of what one hears is true, it shows that Bihar has forgotten humanity," he wrote to Nehru.[5]

Thousands of Hindus and Muslims died in the violence. Mosques were burned and Hindu temples were destroyed. Gandhi walked from village to village, urging Hindus and Muslims to make peace. Gandhi stopped in Calcutta in August to protect Muslims from Hindu violence, but his pleas for calm and order went unheeded.

Gandhi told friends at a prayer breakfast in 1946 that he felt powerless to unite the nation. No one listened to him anymore, he said. "I am crying in the wilderness," lamented Gandhi.[6]

The Great Migration

Meanwhile, the partition of India and Pakistan was under way. Jinnah became the first governor-general of Pakistan, and Mountbatten became the first governor-general of an independent India. Tragically, even Jinnah could not have predicted the chaos that erupted as masses of refugees tried to escape to safety on either side of the new borders. Jinnah died in September 1948 of tuberculosis, leaving a lack of leadership in Pakistan.

More than 10 million people were forced to migrate during the partition of India. Hindus in Islamic Pakistan abandoned their homes and jobs to flee to India. Muslims whose families had been Indian for generations escaped to Pakistan for their lives. Families were torn apart. Many Hindus and Sikhs who remained in Pakistan converted to Islam to save their property and businesses. The refugees' journeys were perilous. For probably one million people or more, the journey ended in death. Trainloads of refugees were

Refugees get on a train during the partition of India. During the scramble to move to the nation of their choice, many people were killed or injured.

massacred by both Hindus and Muslims. Villages were burned.

Gandhi's Last Efforts for Peace

In September 1947, Gandhi arrived in Delhi. The city was in chaos. It was choked with partition refugees. Mobs were burning and looting those Muslim families who tried to stay in Delhi. In one refugee camp, some seventy-five thousand Muslims were waiting to be moved to Pakistan. In October, Gandhi turned seventy-eight. Frail and ill with a persistent cough, he was still determined to bring peace.

On January 13, 1948, Gandhi announced his last fast to reconcile Hindus and Muslims. He refused to eat for five days. Once again, the people reacted to his pleas, and the city calmed. But Gandhi had enemies. Some Hindus felt he sympathized too strongly with the Muslims. At his prayer meetings, he read passages from the Koran and criticized Hindus for burning Muslim mosques. "Death to Gandhi!" became the cry of some Hindu extremists. On January 20, an explosion in the garden outside the house where

Source Document

I will give you a talisman [lucky charm]. Whenever you are in doubt, or when the self becomes too much with you, apply the following test. Recall the face of the poorest and the weakest man whom you may have seen, and ask yourself, if the step you contemplate is going to be of any use to him. Will he gain anything by it? Will it restore him to a control over his own life and destiny? In other words will it lead to Swaraj for the hungry and spiritually starving millions? Then you will find your doubts and your self melting away.[7]

One of the last notes signed by Gandhi in 1948.

Gandhi was staying was found to be an assassination attempt by Hindu extremists. In a dark premonition, Gandhi told his friends, "If I fall victim to an assassin's bullet, there must be no anger within me."[8]

Gandhi's Final Hours

On January 30, 1948, Gandhi began his day as usual. He woke at 3:30 A.M. to work on a draft of the new Indian Constitution. Then he met with his old friend, Vallabhbhai Patel. Just after 5:00 P.M., he set out for his daily prayer meeting in the garden, accompanied by two grandnieces, Manubehn and Abhabehn.

Wearing a white woolen shawl, Gandhi walked across the grass and climbed the steps to the terrace, where a crowd was waiting. As he met the crowd, he stood and folded his hands in the traditional Hindu greeting.

A man suddenly pushed through the crowd. He bent his head respectfully before Gandhi, then fired three shots at him. Gandhi cried out, "Hai Rama! Hai Rama!" (Oh God!).[9] His hands were still folded together. Gandhi died immediately in the laps of the two girls.

His assassin, a young Hindu extremist named Nathauram Godse, the editor of a Hindu nationalist newspaper in Poona, was quickly arrested. He had not acted alone. A band of young Hindus had been planning Gandhi's assassination for months. Eight men were later tried for conspiracy. Godse and an associate, Narayan Apte, were executed for the crime on November 15, 1949.

India Says Farewell

Gandhi's body was laid on the floor at Birla House. His son Devadas came quickly, as did Nehru. To stop rumors that a Muslim had killed Gandhi, All-India Radio promptly informed the nation: "Mahatma Gandhi was assassinated in New Delhi at twenty minutes past five this afternoon. His assassin was a Hindu."[10]

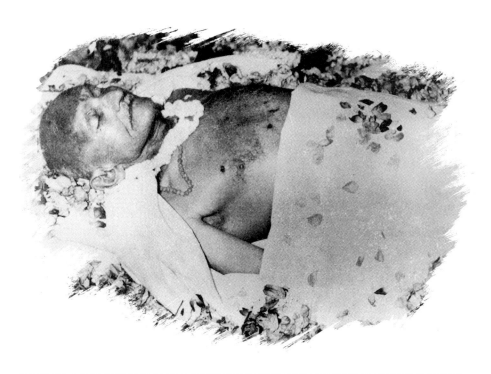

Gandhi's body is seen here lying in state on January 31, 1948. Thousands filed past to see the great leader one last time.

The news of Gandhi's murder traveled fast. In the gardens and nearby streets, thousands of people gathered. They sobbed and chanted, *"Mahatma Gandhi ki jai"* (Mahatma Gandhi, to him victory).[11]

That evening, Nehru spoke to a grieving nation over All-India Radio. "The light has gone out of our lives and there is darkness everywhere and I do not quite know what to tell you and how to say it," said Nehru. "Our beloved leader, Bapu [affectionate word for father] as we called him, the father of our nation, is no more."[12]

The following day, Gandhi's body was prepared for cremation. To symbolize purification, a vermilion mark was painted on his forehead, his rosary and a garland of hand-spun yarn were placed around his neck, and he was anointed with sandalwood paste. Then Gandhi's body was lifted onto a platform on an army truck. The Indian flag was draped over his body.

The funeral procession set off down the boulevards to the Delhi Gate and the Jumna River. Thousands of government troops, police, Gandhi's workers, and political leaders, including Nehru, Patel, and Lord Mountbatten, accompanied the truck. Perhaps a million people choked the streets to catch a last glimpse of the fallen leader. Indian Air Force planes dropped roses on the mourners.

Late in the afternoon, the army truck reached the cremation site, a small brick platform next to the river. The body was laid on the platform and sprinkled with holy water, and sandalwood logs were arranged over

Gandhi's funeral pyre.

it. A priest recited the sacred mantras, or Hindu prayers, as the crowd pressed against the barricades. Gandhi's third son, Ramdas, lit the funeral pyre. As the flames rose into the sky, the crowd shouted, *"Mahatmaji amar ho gae,"* meaning, "Mahatmaji has become immortal."[13]

Thirteen days later, Gandhi's bones were gathered and scattered in the waters at Allahabad, at the Trivenie, the Hindus' sacred meeting place of three rivers: the Ganges, the Jumna, and the invisible celestial river. His ashes were sprinkled in sacred waters across India. Gandhi's estranged son, Harilal, visited the cremation ground afterward. He died of tuberculosis in a Bombay hospital less than five months later.

The only positive result of Gandhi's assassination was that the religious disorder suddenly ended. Abruptly, the saddened nation was shakily at peace.

The World Grieves

All the world mourned the death of Gandhi. The United Nations in New York City lowered its flag to half-mast. Condolence messages poured into India.

The British representative in the United Nations, Philip Noel-Baker, praised Gandhi as "the friend of the poorest and the loneliest and the lost."[14] United States President Harry Truman praised Gandhi for his "selfless struggle for the betterment of his people."[15]

Lord Mountbatten expressed the hope that Gandhi's life might "inspire our troubled world to save itself by following his noble example."[16] American physicist Albert Einstein wrote, "Generations to come, it may be, will scarce believe that such a one as

Source Document

The light has gone out, I said, and yet I was wrong. For the light that shone in this country was no ordinary light. The light that has illumined this country for these many years will illumine this country for many more years, and a thousand years later that light will still be seen in this country, and the world will see it and it will give solace to innumerable hearts. For that light represented the living truth, and the eternal man was with us with his eternal truth reminding us of the right path, drawing us from error, taking this country to freedom.[17]

Nehru, speaking on All-India Radio following the death of Mahatma Gandhi.

this ever in flesh and blood walked upon this earth."[18] Even Gandhi's adversary, Sir Stafford Cripps, praised the Mahatma: "I know no other man of any time or indeed in recent history who so forcefully and convincingly demonstrated the power of spirit over material things."[19]

A New Beginning

India had been ruled for eight centuries by sultans, emperors, and British viceroys and civil servants. For the first time, India controlled its own future. On January 26, 1950, India adopted a new constitution and became an independent democratic republic. The first general election was held in 1952.

Nehru was elected prime minister, a position he held until his death in 1964. Dr. Rajendra Prasad, a disciple of Gandhi's and a leader of the Indian National Congress, was India's first president. The prime minister is the leader of the political party that has the most seats in the Indian Parliament. The president, with fewer powers, is elected by Parliament.

The Indian Constitution, which was based on the constitutions of the United States, Great Britain, and other Western countries, established a secular, or nonreligious, nation with a parliamentary system of government and democratic ideals. As Gandhi had wished, untouchability was outlawed. However, discrimination against untouchables still persists today. The constitution also provided civil rights such as free speech and freedom of assembly, and equal rights for women and minorities. All adults were given the right to vote. The princely states ruled by the maharajas were soon brought into the nation of India.

In the next decades, Nehru led India in a series of five-year economic plans. He oversaw the construction of steel plants, oil refineries, hydroelectric complexes, and the modernization of agriculture. He followed a policy of nonalignment, or independence from the world's superpowers. (After World War II, most countries of the world allied with either the United States or the Communist Soviet Union.) Nehru also advocated peaceful coexistence with India's neighbors. He encouraged women to become educated and employed. Following his death, his daughter, Indira Gandhi, served as prime minister from 1966 to 1977, and again in 1980 to 1984.

Partition created a border of hatred between Pakistan and India. They fought two wars over the disputed territory of Kashmir, the predominantly Muslim state next to Pakistan, in 1947 and 1965. In 1971, civil war broke out between East and West Pakistan. India sided with East Pakistan. In December 1971, West Pakistan was defeated and East Pakistan became Bangladesh, one of the world's poorest nations.

Since gaining independence in 1947, Pakistan, with a population of 150 million people in the year 2000, has alternated between civilian and military governments. Pakistani leaders have been plagued by charges of corruption. A military coup in October 1999 overthrew the elected government, ending ten years of democracy and leaving the nearly bankrupt nation under the rule of army officers.

Relations between India and Pakistan remain troubled. After both nations conducted nuclear weapons tests in 1998, the two nations' prime ministers met in Lahore, Pakistan, in February 1999 to take steps toward reconciliation. But the neighbors that share so much history are still embroiled in their dispute over Kashmir, and there is international concern that nuclear war could one day erupt in the region. American President Bill Clinton made a historic visit to India, Pakistan, and Bangladesh in March 2000 to help bring Pakistan and India closer together and to strengthen ties between South Asia and the United States.

The nation that was born out of Gandhi's message of peace has been scarred by violence since his death. In 1984, Prime Minister Indira Gandhi was assassinated by one of her bodyguards, a member of an extremist Sikh group. Her son, Rajiv, became her successor. He, too, was assassinated, in May 1991. Rajiv's wife, Sonia Gandhi, an Italian-born Catholic, was elected president of the opposition Congress party in 1998. The Congress party, which began as the Indian National Congress, is a major political party in modern democratic India.

India in the New Millennium

With a population of a billion people, India faces serious challenges, many related to poverty. "It has more than 320 million abjectly [wretchedly] poor people unable to muster an income equivalent to the $1 a day that is needed to buy basic foods," wrote Barbara Crossette in *The New York Times* in August 1999.[20] In 1997, the United Nations International Children's Fund reported that more than 53 percent of India's children under the age of five suffer from malnutrition. One third of New Delhi's 10 million residents live in unsanitary slum areas with poor access to water and health care. Education is out of reach for millions of children, whose families cannot afford clothes or school supplies. Only about 66 percent of males and 38 percent of females ages fifteen and over can read and write.

Religious and caste divisions have deepened in recent decades. Thousands of Sikhs were jailed during a Sikh separatist uprising in the Punjab. The Sikhs have long demanded their own independent nation in the Punjab. However, the uprising was crushed in the early 1990s. Anti-Muslim riots flared in Bombay in the 1990s. In 1998 and 1999, Hindu extremists murdered Christians in a series of rampages.

Despite legal protections, India's untouchables still fight for basic rights and dignity. They are barred from public drinking water in some villages and forced to take the lowest jobs. Yet with the help of government quotas in education and employment, thousands of untouchables have broken through social barriers to achieve higher education and professional status. In 1997, Kicheril Raman Narayanan, an untouchable, was elected India's president.

India's Riches

Fueled by its plentiful natural resources and large workforce, India has become a major industrial power since independence. Economic reforms in the early 1990s allowed India to attract multinational corporations—giant companies with branches in many foreign countries. India is a leading exporter of rice, tea, jute (the woody herb used to make twine, burlap, and paper), and computer hardware and software. The nation is also an innovator in the fields of nuclear energy, satellite launching, missile technology, and medicine.

Despite constant political turmoil, India remains the world's largest democracy. Gandhi's Congress party is still powerful. Many of India's ancient traditions survive. Although India is secular, it is a deeply religious country. Indian art, music, and architecture continue to draw tourists from around the world.

Epilogue

India might well have won independence without Gandhi. Nehru and other congress leaders also inspired and led India's long journey to end colonial rule. After World War II, Great Britain was ready to give up its colonies. However, Gandhi's satyagraha gave India's freedom movement an extraordinary quality.

American journalist William Shirer, who went to India in 1930 to report on Gandhi, observed that the Mahatma "taught us all that there was a greater power

Martin Luther King, Jr., was one of many civil rights leaders influenced by Mahatma Gandhi's peaceful tactics.

in life than force, which seemed to have ruled the planet since men first sprouted on it. That power lay in the spirit, in Truth and love, in non-violent action."[21]

Gandhi inspired countless individuals to follow his teachings. In South Africa, the struggle for racial equality took many decades. Influenced in part by Gandhi's political organizing in Natal, South Africans founded the South African Native National Congress in 1912. The African National Congress, as it came to be known, pressed for equal rights for all Africans. But life for blacks and Indians in South Africa worsened when the segregated police state of apartheid began in 1946. After a long struggle, in 1996, President Nelson Mandela, a leader of the African National Congress and an admirer of Gandhi, signed a new constitution. Finally, all South Africans, regardless of race, were guaranteed freedom of religion, expression, the press, and political activity. They also won the right to adequate housing, food, water, education, and health care. South Africa's long journey to end legalized racial segregation and discrimination was over.

In the United States, the Reverend Martin Luther King, Jr., adopted Gandhi's methods in the fight for civil rights for African Americans. While others urged violence to fight racial discrimination, King, who studied Gandhi's writings, maintained that noncooperation and peaceful resistance such as boycotts and sit-ins were better weapons. "The Gandhian method of nonviolent resistance . . . became the guiding light of our movement. Christ furnished the spirit and motivation and Gandhi furnished the method," King wrote.[22] Tragically, in 1968, King, like Gandhi, was killed by an assassin's bullet.

Indian independence was only part of Gandhi's dream for India. He also wanted Indians to welcome untouchables into their homes, and he hoped for peace between Hindus and Muslims. Gandhi envisioned an India where all people would be treated with respect and dignity. He tried to improve the lives of the poorest Indians, and he inspired others to practice humility and kindness. As General George C. Marshall, the United States secretary of state from 1946 to 1949, said at Gandhi's death, "Mahatma Gandhi was the spokesman for the conscience of mankind."[23]

Gandhi is still remembered for his commitment to nonviolence and peaceful change.

Timeline

1500 B.C.—Aryan tribes invade India and settle in the Punjab region.

A.D. **1175 –1200**—Islamic invaders enter northern India.

1498—Portuguese explorer Vasco de Gama sails into Kozhikode.

1526—The Mughal Empire is established.

1600—Queen Elizabeth I signs the charter for the East India Company.

1690—The English settle Calcutta.

1757—Battle of Plassey establishes British dominance in India.

1773—The East India Company begins to govern directly in Bengal.

1857—The Sepoy Rebellion erupts and is crushed by the British a year later.

1858—The British government takes over the rule of India.

1869—*October 2*: Mohandas Karamchand Gandhi is born.

1882—Gandhi marries Kasturbhai Makanji.

1885—The Indian National Congress is founded.

1888—Gandhi's first son, Harilal, is born; Gandhi sails for England to study law.

1891—Gandhi becomes a lawyer and returns to India.

1893—Gandhi sails to South Africa to work as a lawyer.

1894—Gandhi creates the Natal Indian Congress.

1899—Gandhi organizes Indian Ambulance Corps during Boer War.

1906—The Muslim League is founded in India.

1908—Gandhi is imprisoned for failing to register under the Black Act.

1909—Gandhi writes *Hind Swaraj* on the boat from London to India, setting out his ideas about Indian independence.

1914—*January*: Gandhi and General Jan Smuts begin negotiations, resulting in more rights for Indians in South Africa.

1914 –1918—World War I is fought.

1915—*January 9*: Gandhi returns to India.

1917—Gandhi helps indigo workers in Champaran.

1919—*April 13*: British forces kill more than four hundred Indians and wound over twelve hundred in the massacre at Amritsar.

1920 –1922—Gandhi leads the Indian National Congress and introduces nonviolent disobedience.

1930 –1931—Gandhi leads Salt March.

1931—Gandhi goes to the Round Table Conferences in London.

1930s—Gandhi launches the Harijan movement.

1935—The Government of India Act gives one sixth of the population the right to vote and outlines a framework for self-government for India.

1939 –1945—World War II is fought.

1940—The Muslim League demands an Islamic nation of Pakistan.

1942—The Cripps Mission fails; Indian National Congress passes "Quit India" resolution on August 8.

1944—*February 22*: Kasturbhai dies in prison.

1946—Hindu-Muslim violence in Bengal.

1947—*March 22*: Lord Mountbatten arrives in India.

1947 –1948—*August 14–15*: British India is divided into the independent states of Pakistan and India; Jawaharlal Nehru becomes India's new prime minister.

1947—*August–September*: Massacres in the Punjab.

1948—*January 30*: Gandhi is assassinated.

1950—*January 26*: India's new constitution is adopted.

1952—India's first democratic elections take place.

Chapter Notes

Chapter 1. The Salt March

1. Quoted in Dennis Dalton, *Mahatma Gandhi: Nonviolent Power in Action* (New York: Columbia University Press, 1993), p. 115.

2. Quoted in Louis Fischer, *The Life of Mahatma Gandhi* (New York: Harper & Row, 1950, 1983), p. 265.

3. *Itihaas: Gandhiji's Writing*, n.d., <http://www.itihaas.com/modern/gandhi-writing.html> (April 6, 1999).

Chapter 2. Europe Discovers India

1. Rudrangshu Mukherjee, ed., *The Penguin Gandhi Reader* (New York: Penguin Books, 1993), p. 223.

2. Quoted in Editors of Time-Life Books, *India* (Alexandria, Va.: Time-Life Books, 1987), p. 15.

3. Louis Fischer, *Gandhi: His Life and Message for the World* (New York: Penguin Books, 1954, 1982), p. 61.

Chapter 3. Gandhi's Early Years

1. Mohandas K. Gandhi, *Autobiography: The Story of My Experiments With Truth* (New York: Dover Publications, 1983), p. 1.

2. Ibid., p. 2.

3. Ibid., p. 3.

4. Louis Fischer, *Gandhi: His Life and Message for the World* (New York: Penguin Books, 1954, 1982), p. 9.

5. Gandhi, p. 20.

6. Ibid., p. 2.

7. Ibid.

8. Ibid., p. 6.

9. Ibid., p. 17.

10. Fischer, p. 14.

11. Judith M. Brown, *Gandhi, Prisoner of Hope* (New Haven: Yale University Press, 1989), p. 30.

Chapter 4. Fighting for Civil Rights in South Africa

1. Mohandas K. Gandhi, *Autobiography: The Story of My Experiments With Truth* (New York: Dover Publications, 1983), p. 97.

2. Ibid.

3. Ibid., p. 114.

4. Louis Fischer, *Gandhi: His Life and Message for the World* (New York: Penguin Books, 1954, 1983), p. 25.

5. Gandhi, p. 167.

6. Ibid., p. 162.

7. Robert Payne, *The Life and Death of Mahatma Gandhi* (New York: E. P. Dutton & Co., 1969), p. 163.

8. Fischer, p. 52.

Chapter 5. The Indian National Congress

1. Vincent A. Smith, *The Oxford History of India*, 4th ed. (Calcutta: Oxford University Press, 1981, 1997), p. 735.

2. Lawrence James, *Raj: The Making and Unmaking of British India* (New York: St. Martin's Press, 1999), p. 420.

3. Ibid., p. 311.

4. Ibid., p. 174.

5. Rudyard Kipling, *Kim* (New York: Alfred A. Knopf, 1995), p. 133.

6. Jabez T. Sunderland, "The New Nationalist Movement in India," *The Atlantic Monthly*, n.d., <http://www.theatlantic.com/issues/08oct/nationmo.htm> (April 11, 2000).

Chapter 6. Rebellion and Reform

1. Judith M. Brown, *Gandhi, Prisoner of Hope* (New Haven: Yale University Press, 1989), p. 97.

2. Quoted in Robert Payne, *The Life and Death of Mahatma Gandhi* (New York: E. P. Dutton & Co., 1969), p. 309.

3. Geoffrey Ashe, *Gandhi* (New York: Stein and Day, 1968), p. 166.

4. Payne, p. 319.

5. Quoted in Louis Fischer, *Gandhi: His Life and Message for the World* (New York: Penguin Books, 1954, 1982), p. 69.

6. Ibid., p. 97.

7. Mohandas K. Gandhi, *Autobiography: The Story of My Experiments With Truth* (New York: Dover Publications, 1983), p. 454.

8. Quoted in Payne, p. 364.

9. Brown, p. 104.

10. Vincent A. Smith, *The Oxford History of India*, 4th ed. (Calcutta: Oxford University Press, 1981), p. 786.

Chapter 7. The Spinning Wheel and Nehru

1. Quoted in Louis Fischer, *Gandhi: His Life and Message for the World* (New York: Penguin Books, 1954, 1982), p. 132.

2. Mohandas K. Gandhi, *Autobiography: The Story of My Experiments With Truth* (New York: Dover Publications, 1983), p. 441.

3. R. K. Narayan, *Swami and Friends* (Chicago: University of Chicago Press, 1980), p. 97.

4. Mohandas K. Gandhi, *Mahatma: A Golden Treasury of Wisdom, Thoughts & Glimpses of Life* (Bombay: India Printing Works, 1995), p. 36.

5. Ibid., p. 64.

6. John F. Burns, "Gandhi Off the Pedestal: All Too Human Parent As Well As Great Guru," *The New York Times*, May 2, 1998, p. B9.

7. Judith M. Brown, *Gandhi, Prisoner of Hope* (New Haven: Yale University Press, 1989), p. 149.

8. Quoted in Stanley Wolpert, *Nehru: A Tryst with Destiny* (New York: Oxford University Press, 1996), p. 167.

9. Quoted in James Traub, *India: The Challenge of Change* (New York: Julian Messner, 1985), p. 114.

Chapter 8. Quit India

1. Quoted in Larry Collins and Dominique LaPierre, *Freedom at Midnight* (New York: Simon and Schuster, 1975), p. 59.

2. William L. Shirer, *Gandhi: A Memoir* (New York: Simon and Schuster, 1979), p. 55.

3. Quoted in Robert Payne, *The Life and Death of Mahatma Gandhi* (New York: E. P. Dutton & Co., 1969), p. 605.

4. Ibid., p. 444.

5. Ibid., p. 486.

6. Ibid., p. 493; Quoted in Collins and LaPierre, p. 63.

7. Quoted in Payne, p. 495.

8. Ibid., p. 502.

9. Quoted in Rudrangshu Mukherjee, ed., *The Penguin Gandhi Reader* (New York: Penguin Books, 1996), p. 271.

10. Stanley Wolpert, *Nehru: A Tryst with Destiny* (New York: Oxford University Press, 1996), p. 383.

11. Ibid.

12. Quoted in Vincent A. Smith, *The Oxford History of India*, 4th ed. (Calcutta: Oxford University Press, 1981), p. 832.

Chapter 9. A New Nation and the Death of Gandhi

1. Larry Collins and Dominique LaPierre, *Freedom at Midnight* (New York: Simon and Schuster, 1975), p. 275.

2. Stanley Wolpert, *Nehru: A Tryst with Destiny* (New York: Oxford University Press, 1996), p. 406.

3. Lawrence James, *Raj: The Making and Unmaking of British India* (New York: St. Martin's Press, 1999), p. 641.

4. Wolpert, p. 406.

5. Quoted in Geoffrey Ashe, *Gandhi* (New York: Stein and Day, 1968), p. 365.

6. Quoted in Judith M. Brown, *Gandhi, Prisoner of Hope* (New Haven: Yale University Press, 1989), p. 369.

7. Quoted in Dennis Dalton, *Mahatma Gandhi: Nonviolent Power in Action* (New York: Columbia University Press, 1993), (photo section between pp. 138 and 139).

8. Quoted in Catherine Bush, *Gandhi* (New York: Chelsea House Publishers, 1985), p. 98.

9. Quoted in Robert Payne, *The Life and Death of Mahatma Gandhi* (New York: E. P. Dutton & Co., 1969), p. 590.

10. Collins and LaPierre, p. 454.

11. Payne, p. 593.

12. Quoted in Payne, p. 595.

13. Ibid., p. 598.

14. Quoted in Louis Fischer, *The Life of Mahatma Gandhi* (New York: Harper & Row, 1950, 1983), pp. 10–11.

15. Quoted in Payne, p. 601.

16. Fischer, p. 11.

17. Quoted in Payne, p. 595.

18. William L. Shirer, *Gandhi: A Memoir* (New York: Simon and Schuster, 1979), p. 11.

19. Fischer, p. 12.

20. Barbara Crossette, "In Days, India, Chasing China, Will Have a Billion People," *The New York Times*, August 5, 1999, p. A10.

21. Shirer, p. 245.

22. Shashi Tharoor, *India: From Midnight to the Millennium* (New York: HarperPerennial, 1998), p. 19.

23. Quoted in Louis Fischer, *Gandhi: His Life and Message for the World* (New York: Penguin Books, 1954, 1982), p. 8.

Further Reading

Books

Bush, Catherine. *Gandhi.* New York: Chelsea House, 1985.

Gandhi, Mohandas K. *Autobiography: The Story of My Experiments With Truth.* New York: Dover Publications, 1983.

Kipling, Rudyard. *Kim.* New York: Alfred A. Knopf, 1995.

McNair, Sylvia. *India: Enchantment of the World.* Chicago: Children's Press, 1990.

Narayan, R. K. *Swami and Friends.* Chicago: The University of Chicago Press, 1944, 1980.

Severance, John B. *Gandhi: Great Soul.* New York: Clarion Books, 1997.

Sheehan, Sean. *Pakistan.* New York: Marshall Cavendish, 1994.

Srinivasan, Tadhika. *India.* New York: Marshall Cavendish, 1990.

Traub, James. *India: The Challenge of Change.* New York: Messner, 1981, 1985.

Wangu, Madhu Baza. *Hinduism.* New York: Facts on File, 1991.

Internet Addresses

Ministry of External Affairs of the Government of India. *Discover India.* September 12, 1999. <http://www.indiagov.org> (September 21, 1999).

M.K. Gandhi Institute for Nonviolence. April 3, 1999. <http://www.cbu.edu/Gandhi> (September 21, 1999).

Times of India. September 21, 1999. <http://www.timesofindia.com> (September 21, 1999).

Washington Post. 1997. <http://www.washingtonpost.com/wp-srv/inatl/asia/aug/15anniversary.htm> (September 21, 1999).

Welcome to India. 1997. <http://www.welcometoindia.com> (September 21, 1999).

Index

A

Act for the Better
Government of India,
23–24
Ahmedabad textile strike, 68
Amritsar Massacre, 70–71
Attlee, Clement, 96

B

Black Act, 47–48, 49
Boers, 39, 41, 43–44, 48, 49
Botha, Louis, 44
British Commonwealth of
Nations, 76, 91, 103–104
British East India Company,
12–13, 21, 22, 24
British Empire, 5, 24–27, 76,
86, 88, 103
British Raj, 5, 57–61, 74–75,
85

C

caste system, 19, 20
Churchill, Winston, 85–86
Cripps, Sir Stafford, 91, 113

D

Dyer, Reginald, 70–71

G

Gandhi, Devadas, 45, 109
Gandhi, Harilal, 34, 45, 82,
111
Gandhi, Indira, 115
Gandhi, Karamchand, 28, 30,
34

Gandhi, Kasturbhai, 33–34,
45, 46–47, 52, 54, 77,
93–94, 95
Gandhi, Manilal, 45
Gandhi, Mohandas K.
asceticism, 80–82
assassination, 108–109
birth, 28
childhood, 30, 31–32
fasting, 86–87, 88
funeral, 110–111
Hinduism, 31–32
imprisonment in Yeravda
jail, 74, 86–87
joins Indian National
Congress, 67
law studies, 34–35
legacy, 117–119
marriage, 32, 33–34
Salt March, 5
spinning, 78–80
Gandhi, Putlibai, 30, 32, 33
Gandhi, Rajiv, 115
Gandhi, Ramdas, 45
Gandhi, Sonia, 115
Gandhi, Uttamchand, 30
Godse, Nathauram, 108
Gokhale, Gopal Krishna,
55–56

H

Hind Swaraj, 50
Hinduism, 15–16, 22–23,
31–32, 58
Hindu-Muslim unrest, 61–62,
95–96, 104–105, 107

Hitler, Adolf, 89, 90

I

India
  Constitution, 108, 113–114
  first democratic election,
    113
  geography, 13–14
  language, 14
  modern India, 115–117
  religion, 15–17, 18–19
Indian Ambulance Corps, 43
Indian Civil Service, 57–58
Indian independence, 100,
  102–104, 113–114
Indian National Congress, 54,
  67–68, 76, 79, 80, 86, 89,
  90–91
Indigo Rebellion, 65–67
Irwin, Lord Edward Wood, 8,
  10, 85, 86

J

Jainism, 17, 18
Jinnah, Mohammed Ali, 63,
  95, 98–99

K

Khilafat Movement, 71–72

M

Macaulay, Lord Thomas, 21
maharajas, 13, 21, 24, 26, 88
Mandela, Nelson, 118
Marshall, George C., 119
Montagu-Chelmsford
  Reforms, 75
Montagu, Edwin, 74–75
Morley-Minto Reforms of
  1909, 61
Mountbatten, Lord Louis,
  96,97, 98–99, 100, 104, 112
Muslim League, 62, 63, 91,
  95–96

N

Natal Indian Congress, 42
Nehru, Jawaharlal, 9, 10, 82,
  83–84, 89, 91, 93, 97, 99,
  100, 102, 110, 113, 114, 117
noncooperation, 72–74, 79

P

Pakistan, 95–96, 98–99, 102,
  105, 114–115
partition of India, 99, 105–106,
  114
Patel, Vallabhbhai, 68
Prasad, Rajendra, 113

Q

Quit India, 93

R

Reading, Lord Rufus Isaacs, 73
Rowlatt Acts, 69

S

Salt March, 5–8, 10–11, 85, 88
satyagraha, 49, 51, 117
Sepoy Rebellion, 22–24, 58
Shukla, Rajkumar, 66
Slade, Madeleine, 93
Smuts, Jan Christiaan, 49, 51
South Africa
  apartheid, 118
  colonization, 38–39
  Indian immigrants, 40
Swadeshi Movement, 79–80

T

Tagore, Rabindranath, 71
Tilak, Bal Gangadhar, 56, 67

U

untouchables, 20, 81–82, 113,
  116, 119

W

Willingdon, Lord Freeman, 86
World War I, 51–52, 68–69, 76
World War II, 89–91, 95